The Writings of Frithjof Schuon
Series

World Wisdom
The Library of Perennial Philosophy

The Library of Perennial Philosophy is dedicated to the exposition of the timeless Truth underlying the diverse religions. This Truth, often referred to as the *Sophia Perennis*—or Perennial Wisdom—finds its expression in the revealed Scriptures as well as the writings of the great sages and the artistic creations of the traditional worlds.

Echoes of Perennial Wisdom appears as one of our selections in the Writings of Frithjof Schuon series.

The Writings of Frithjof Schuon

The Writings of Frithjof Schuon form the foundation of our library because he is the pre-eminent exponent of the Perennial Philosophy. His work illuminates this perspective in both an essential and comprehensive manner like none other.

Echoes of
Perennial Wisdom

A New Translation with Selected Letters

by
Frithjof Schuon

Includes Other Previously
Unpublished Writings

Edited by
Patrick Casey

World Wisdom

Echoes of Perennial Wisdom:
A New Translation with Selected Letters
© 2012 World Wisdom, Inc.

Translated by Mark Perry and Jean-Pierre Lafouge

Library of Congress Cataloging-in-Publication Data

Schuon, Frithjof, 1907-1998.
  [Perles du pèlerin. English]
  Echoes of perennial wisdom : a new translation with selected
letters / by Frithjof Schuon ; [translated by Mark Perry and Jean-
Pierre Lafouge] ; edited by Patrick Casey.
      p. cm. -- (The writings of Frithjof Schuon) (The library of
perennial philosophy)
  "Includes other previously unpublished writings."
  Includes bibliographical references.
  ISBN 978-1-936597-00-0 (pbk. : alk. paper) 1. Metaphysics-
-Miscellanea. 2. Religion--Philosophy--Miscellanea. 3. Spiritual
life--Miscellanea. I. Casey, Patrick, 1953- II. Title.
  BD112.S21413 2012
  110--dc23

                                                2011044257

Cover Art: Detail from a painting by Frithjof Schuon

Printed on acid-free paper in the United States of America

For information address World Wisdom, Inc.
P. O. Box 2682, Bloomington, Indiana 47402-2682
www.worldwisdom.com

CONTENTS

Frithjof Schuon, c. 1990

EDITOR'S PREFACE

Frithjof Schuon was a German who wrote almost all his books in French and who acquired Swiss nationality in the French part of Switzerland. To mention this is not superfluous, for Schuon's writings—like those of his spiritual ancestor Meister Eckhart—have the merit of combining German imaginativity and profundity with French precision, clarity, and elegance. Another enriching feature of Schuon's work is the fascinating combination of a rigorous intellectuality with a remarkable artistic sensibility, one might even say: with a kind of mystical musicality.

In his early youth, Schuon's doctrinal starting point was the *Vedānta*; and he was for twenty years the collaborator of the French metaphysician and esoterist René Guénon.

Schuon's message comprises mainly the following fields: essential and hence universal metaphysics, with their cosmological and anthropological ramifications; spirituality in the broadest sense; intrinsic morals and aesthetics; traditional principles and phenomena; Islam in general and Sufism in particular; *Vedānta* and other forms of Eastern wisdom; sacred art.

Let us add that in his youth and again in his last years, Schuon wrote beautiful lyrical poems in his

German mother tongue, and that throughout his whole life he was a very gifted painter; most of his somewhat hieratic paintings deal with the Plains Indians, with whom he has a strong personal connection, having even been officially adopted into the Sioux tribe. Schuon's message is artistic and existential as well as philosophical and intellectual, both modes being possible and fundamental expressions of concrete spirituality.

·:·

With regard to a previous edition of this book, Schuon wrote:

> The form of this collection corresponds to a very particular mode of doctrinal presentation, and thus also to a particular need for spiritual assimilation. At some moments, one may have the inclination to enter into an author's thinking by a conscientious exploration of one of his books; at other times or in other circumstances, one may prefer over this mode of assimilation a less laborious and somehow carefree exploration that could be likened to a meditative stroll in a garden. Such may be the case when one selects something

———— ·⫶· ————

for a travel reading that, without being too demanding, at least does not waste our time; such a reading, though not necessarily easier as regards its subject, can be made lighter by its free-flowing presentation.

. . . There is moreover a precedent—if one may say—for this literary genre found in our book *Spiritual Perspectives and Human Facts;* in this work, the author's thinking is offered, not in the form of articles or of chapters, but in the form of select fragments taken from unpublished papers or letters. It may perhaps be worth mentioning here the fact of our having employed this free and discontinuous style in our very first work, written in German and entitled *Urbesinnung* ("Primordial Meditation"[1]); the themes presented there were taken up in our subsequent French books.

In choosing the fragments that make up the present book, [care was taken] to insert texts, among others, regarding the spiritual life in its simple and concrete aspects so that [it] offers on balance a nourishment from

---

[1] Editor's Note: see Gillian Harris' English translation, "Primordial Meditation: Contemplating the Real", *Sacred Web,* 20, Winter 2007, pp. 19-120.

———— ∴ ————

which no one is excluded; . . . [it being] a spiritual peregrination not limited to metaphysics alone but somehow encompassing "all that is human".

The presentation of this work has nothing systematic about it; longer excerpts have been added at the end of the book because they were discovered later, without it having been considered necessary to classify the texts according to subject matter. A pilgrim passes through a region as it offers itself to his view; be that as it may, spiritual experiences are situated outside of space and time.[2]

∴

This edition of *Echoes of Perennial Wisdom* contains three significant changes from the 1992 version published by World Wisdom. Firstly, unlike the earlier edition, all citations have been sourced, including the many passages from Schuon's *Book of Keys*, a collection of spiritual texts he wrote for his followers.[3]

---

[2] *Les Perles du pèlerin* (Paris: Éditions du Seuil, 1990), pp. 7-8.

[3] "'The Book of Keys' (is) a collection of private spiritual texts written by Schuon for his spiritual community" (*Prayer*

These references have been listed by page number in the editor's notes. Secondly, Schuon wrote primarily in French or German and only occasionally in English; the translators have gone back to the original language for all French and German passages, and retranslated them. In doing so, the translators have also restored the author's use of capitalization, for Schuon often-times placed key terms in upper case to emphasize their importance. Lastly, an appendix has been added, drawn primarily from Schuon's correspondence and other previously unpublished writings.

In his foreword to *The Play of Masks*, Schuon wrote, "Even if our writings had on the average no other result than the restitution, for some, of the saving barque that is prayer, we would owe it to God to

Fashions Man: Frithjof Schuon on the Spiritual Life, ed. James S. Cutsinger [Bloomington, IN: World Wisdom, 2005], p. 239). "Martin Lings . . . explained that these texts form 'a series of messages or instructions concerning the spiritual path . . . set down on behalf of his disciples'" (Michael Fitzgerald, *Frithjof Schuon: Messenger of the Perennial Philosophy* [Bloomington, IN: World Wisdom, 2010], p. 222). "His *Book of Keys*, made up of over one thousand texts of one to three pages, is in itself, by its density and depth, a genuine monument of spiritual, eso-teric, and methodic teaching" (Jean-Baptiste Aymard & Patrick Laude, *Frithjof Schuon: Life and Teachings* [Albany, NY: SUNY, 2004], p. 157).

——— ·:· ———

consider ourselves profoundly satisfied."[4] I have no doubt that the reading of this work will, for some, bring about just such a restoration.

Patrick Casey
Bloomington, Indiana
May 2011

[4] Frithjof Schuon, *The Play of Masks* (Bloomington, IN: World Wisdom Books, 1992), p. vii.

Echoes of
Perennial Wisdom

———— ⋅⋮⋅ ————

The worth of man lies in his consciousness of the Absolute.

⋅⋮⋅

Man is made for what he is able to conceive; the very ideas of absoluteness and transcendence prove both his spiritual nature and the supra-terrestrial character of his destiny.

⋅⋮⋅

In fact, what separates man from divine Reality is but a thin partition: God is infinitely close to man, but man is infinitely far from God. This partition, for man, is a mountain; man stands in front of a mountain which he must remove with his own hands. He digs away the earth, but in vain, the mountain remains; man however goes on digging, in the name of God. And the mountain vanishes. It was never there.

⋅⋮⋅

The paradox of the human condition is that nothing could be more contrary to us than the requirement to transcend ourselves, and yet nothing could be more essentially ourselves than the core of this requirement or the fruit of this self-overcoming.

———— ·⁚· ————

Our deformity implies that our spirit is made of absoluteness, our will of freedom, and our soul of generosity; to dominate oneself and to transcend oneself is to remove the layer of ice or of darkness that imprisons the true nature of man.

·⁚·

One of the keys to understanding our true nature and our ultimate destiny is the fact that the things of this world are never proportionate to the actual range of our intelligence. Our intelligence is made for the Absolute, or else it is nothing. The Absolute alone confers on our intelligence the power to accomplish to the full what it can accomplish and to be wholly what it is. Similarly, in the case of the will, which is no more than a prolongation or complement of the intelligence: the objects it commonly sets out to achieve, or those that life imposes on it, do not measure up to the fullness of its range; only the "divine dimension" can satisfy the thirst for plenitude in our willing or our love.

—— ⫶ ——

Whether we like it or not, we live surrounded by mysteries, which logically and existentially draw us towards transcendence.

⫶

The way towards God always involves an inversion: from outwardness one must pass to inwardness, from multiplicity to unity, from dispersion to concentration, from egoism to detachment, from passion to serenity.

⫶

The world scatters us, and the ego compresses us; God gathers us together and dilates us, He appeases us and delivers us.

⫶

Man yearns for happiness because Beatitude, which is made of beauty and love, is his very substance.

———— ·|· ————

The intelligence may well affirm metaphysical and eschatological truths; the imagination—or the sub-conscious—continues to believe firmly in the world, neither in God nor in the hereafter; every man is *a priori* hypocritical. The path is precisely the passage from natural hypocrisy to spiritual sincerity.

·|·

Man is made for the contemplation of the Infinite, and pleasures, while transmitting something of the Infinite through their effective symbolism, turn the soul away from It in the vast majority of cases—and they do this as a result of our fall. In pleasure, the mind is turned away from the Infinite; it is so to speak engulfed in the finite; and since pleasure calls for repetition, it becomes habitual, so that the forget-ting of God becomes a habit, as does also the cult of vanities. Man absorbed by pleasure becomes plea-sure, he ceases to be himself; the soul is ensnared by the periphery, it is as if deprived of its center.

———— ∴ ————

It is only through deifying inwardness, whatever its price, that man is perfectly in conformity with his nature.

∴

In order to be happy, man must have a center; now this center is above all the Certitude of the One. The greatest calamity is the loss of the center and the abandon of the soul to the caprices of the periphery. To be man is to be at the Center; it is to be Center.

∴

The man who "loves God" is thus one who "dwells in the Inward" and "is oriented towards the Inward"; in other words, he remains motionless in his contemplative inwardness—or his "being", if one prefers—while moving towards his infinite Center. Spiritual immobility is here opposed to the endless movement of external phenomena, while spiritual movement, on the contrary, is opposed to the natural inertia of the fallen soul, to the "hardness of heart" that must be cured by "grace" and "love", whose remedy, that is to say, is everything which softens, transmutes, and transcends the ego.

———— ·ɟ· ————

The soul must withdraw itself from the dispersion of the world; this is the quality of Inwardness. Then the will must vanquish the passivity of life; this is the quality of Actuality. Finally, the mind must transcend the unconsciousness of the ego; this is the quality of Simplicity. To perceive the Substance intellectually, above the uproar of accidents, this is to realize Simplicity. To be one is to be simple; for Simplicity is to the One what Inwardness is to the Center and what Actuality is to the Present.

·ɟ·

Man is capable of conceiving of the Absolute and of willing freely; likewise, and by way of consequence, he is capable of a love exceeding phenomena and opening out on the Infinite, and of an activity having its motive or its object beyond terrestrial interests. The specifically human abilities, or such as are the noblest and most completely human, prove in their own way what their objective is, just as the wings of a bird prove the possibility of flight and hence also the existence of space in which the bird can fly.

—— ⋮ ——

Instead of loving the world, one must be in love with the Inward, which is beyond things, beyond the multiple, beyond existence. Likewise, one must be in love with pure Being, which is beyond action and beyond thought.

⋮

To love God does not mean to cultivate a sentiment—that is to say, something which we enjoy without knowing whether God enjoys it—but rather to eliminate from the soul what prevents God from entering it.

⋮

Love of God is firstly the attachment of the intelligence to the Truth, then the attachment of the will to the Good, and finally the attachment of the soul to the Peace that is given by the Truth and the Good.

⋮

To know God is to love Him, and not to love Him is not to know Him.

———— ⋅⫾⋅ ————

All that we can know, we bear within ourselves, hence that is what we are; and that is why we can know it.

⋅⫾⋅

To claim that knowledge as such can only be relative amounts to saying that human ignorance is absolute.

⋅⫾⋅

Will for the Good and love of the Beautiful are the necessary concomitants of knowledge of the True, and their repercussions are incalculable.

⋅⫾⋅

The beautiful is not what we love and because we love it, but that which by its objective value obliges us to love it.

———— ⋅⁝⋅ ————

Beauty, whatever use man may make of it, fundamentally belongs to its Creator, who through it projects into the world of appearances something of His
Being.

⋅⁝⋅

The perception of beauty, being a rigorous adequation and not a subjective illusion, essentially implies
on the one hand a satisfaction of the intelligence and
on the other hand a sentiment of security, infinity,
and love. It implies security, because beauty is unitive and excludes, by means of a kind of musical
evidence, the fissures of doubt and worry; of infinity, because beauty, by its very musicality, melts all
hardness and limitations thus freeing the soul from its
constrictions, be it only in a minute or remote way;
and of love, because beauty calls forth love, that is to
say it invites to union and hence to unitive extinction.

Beauty, and the love of Beauty, give to the Soul the Happiness to which it aspires by its very nature. If the soul wishes to be happy in an unconditional and permanent fashion, it must bear the Beautiful within itself; now the soul can only do this through realizing Virtue, which we could also term Goodness, or Piety.

·:·

Happiness is religion and character; faith and virtue. It is a fact that man cannot find happiness within his own limits; his very nature condemns him to surpass himself, and in surpassing himself, to free himself.

·:·

To transcend oneself: this is the great imperative of the human condition; and there is another that anticipates it and at the same time prolongs it: to dominate oneself. The noble man is one who dominates himself; the holy man is one who transcends himself. Nobility and holiness are the imperatives of the human state.

Holiness is the sleep of the ego and the wake of the immortal soul—of the ego, fed on sensorial impressions and filled with desires, and of the soul, free and crystallized in God. The moving surface of our being must sleep and must therefore withdraw from images and instincts, whereas the depths of our being must be awake in the consciousness of the Divine, thus lighting up, like a motionless flame, the silence of the holy sleep.

·|·

We are not merely "such and such an ego" plunged in the world and determined by it, we are primarily "the ego as such", which stands before God and is determined by Him.

·|·

Sanctity is essentially contemplativity: it is the intuition of the spiritual nature of things; profound intuition which determines the entire soul, hence the entire being of man.

For the sage every star, every flower, is metaphysically a proof of the Infinite.

·⫶·

When God is removed from the universe, it becomes a desert of rocks or ice; it is deprived of life and warmth, and every man who still has a sense of the integrally real refuses to admit that this should be reality; for if reality were made of rocks, there would be no place in it for flowers or any beauty or sweetness whatsoever. Similarly for the soul: remove faith—including that element of faith that forms part of gnosis—and the soul becomes impoverished, chilled, rigid, and embittered; or it falls into a hedonism unworthy of the human state; moreover, the one does not preclude the other, for blind passions always overlay a heart of ice, all told, a heart that is "dead".

·⫶·

This is the great absurdity: that people live without faith and in an inhumanly horizontal manner, in a world where all that nature offers testifies to the supernatural, to the hereafter, to the divine; to eternal spring.

Faith is to say "yes" to God. When man says "yes" to God, God says "yes" to man.

·⁝·

Goodness is in the very substance of the Universe, and for that reason it penetrates right into the matter we know, "accursed" though that matter may be; the fruits of the earth and the rain from the sky, which make life possible, are nothing if not manifestations of the Goodness which penetrates everywhere and warms the world, and which we carry within ourselves, in the depths of our chilled hearts.

·⁝·

Faith as such does not result from our thought, it is before it; it is even before us. In faith we are outside time.

·⁝·

The divine archetype of faith is the "yes" which God says to Himself; it is the Logos which on the one hand mirrors the Divine Infinity, and on the other hand refracts it.

———— ⋅⋮⋅ ————

If faith is a mystery, it is because its nature is inexpressible to the degree that it is profound, for it is not
possible to convey fully by words this vision that is
still blind, and this blindness that already sees.

⋅⋮⋅

The unbeliever, on earth, believes only what he sees;
the believer, in Heaven, sees all that he believes.

⋅⋮⋅

Faith without Truth is heresy; Knowledge without
Faith is hypocrisy. Work without Virtue is pride, and
Virtue without Work is vanity.

⋅⋮⋅

There is no access to the Heart without the virtues.

⋅⋮⋅

Virtue is a ray of the divine Beauty, in which we participate through our nature or through our will, with
ease or with difficulty, but always by the grace of
God.

God does not at the outset ask perfection of us, but He does ask of us its intention, which implies, if it is sincere, the absence of serious imperfection; it is only too obvious that a proud man cannot aspire sincerely to humility. God asks of us that which He has given us, namely the qualities we bear in our own depths, in our deiform substance; man must "become what he is"; every being is fundamentally Being as such.

⋅⫶⋅

Virtue is the conformity of the soul to the divine Model and to the spiritual work; conformity or participation. The essence of the virtues is emptiness before God, which permits the divine Qualities to enter the heart and radiate in the soul. Virtue is the exteriorization of the pure heart.

⋅⫶⋅

Virtue consists in allowing free passage, in the soul, to the Beauty of God.

—— ⁙ ——

To strive for perfection: not because we wish to be perfect for our own glory, but because perfection is beautiful and imperfection ugly; or because virtue is self-evident—that is to say, in conformity with the Real.

⁙

One must beware of any materialistic and demagogic conception of charity and never forget that what "interests" God—and the sole thing that can "interest" Him—is the eternal life of him who gives and the eternal life of him who receives. True charity—we might call it "integral charity"—gives nothing without giving inwardly something better; the art of giving requires that to the material gift should be added a gift of the soul: this is to forget the gift after having given it, and this forgetfulness is like a fresh gift. Intrinsically, that virtue alone is good which is in a certain way unconscious of itself and, as a result, becomes neither "egoistic charity" nor "proud humility".

The first act of charity is to rid the soul of illusions and passions and thus rid the world of a maleficent being; it is to make a void so that God may fill it and, by this fullness, give Himself. A saint is a void open for the passage of God.

∴

To give oneself to God is to give God to the world.

∴

Virtue cut off from God becomes pride, as beauty cut off from God becomes idol; and virtue attached to God becomes sanctity, as beauty attached to God becomes sacrament.

∴

To acquire a quality is to vanquish a fault. To be able to acquire a quality, one must understand it, love it, practice it. To vanquish a fault, one must understand it, detest it, avoid it.

By eliminating vices, we permit God's virtues to penetrate into our soul; it could also be said that it is we who enter into virtue. Do not believe that "it is I who am the virtue"; do not personalize it. The humble man is attached to virtue as such, and consequently to the sentiment that all virtue comes from God and belongs to God.

⁝

Every virtue is a participation in the Beauty of the One and a response to His Love.

⁝

At the bottom of all the vices is found pride; Virtue is essentially consciousness of the nature of things, which situates the ego in its proper place.

On the one hand, one has to resign oneself to being what one is, and on the other hand one has to become a place of the Divine Presence. Every "I" can in principle be a vehicle of the Self, and thereby be free, to a sufficient extent, from contingency.

On the one hand, one has to resign oneself to being where one is, and on the other hand, one has to turn this place into a center through the Remembrance of God; for wherever God is evoked, wherever He is manifested, there is the Center.

On the one hand, one has to resign oneself to living in the moment in which one lives, and on the other hand one has to turn this moment into an Eternal Present, which every present moment becomes through the Remembrance of God; for when God is evoked, when He is manifested, we are in Eternity.

I am myself, and not someone else; and I am here, such as I am; and this necessarily occurs now. What must I do?

The first thing that is obligatory, and the only thing that is obligatory in an absolute fashion, is my relationship with God. I remember God, and in and through this remembrance, all is well, because this remembrance is God's. Everything else lies in His hands.

⋅⁝⋅

There is always a presence in the soul. The most ordinary presence is that of the world, to the exclusion, alas, of that of God. The presence of the world always implies that of the "I"; but sometimes the presence of the "I" is even stronger than that of the world, to the point of occupying the entire space of the soul.

What is the Remembrance of God? It is to offer the space of our soul to the divine Presence, by means, precisely, of the Name of God. To allow God to enter into our space, in order that God may allow us to enter into His space; to welcome Him here below, in order that He may welcome us in the Hereafter, and in a certain manner already in the here-below.

———— ·⁝· ————

One must guard against latent individualism, against the too individual desire to be perfect and the too individual disappointment of not being so. One must aspire to God in an impersonal way.

·⁝·

Spiritual realization is theoretically the easiest thing and in practice the most difficult thing there is. It is the easiest because it is enough to think of God; it is the most difficult because human nature is forgetfulness of God.

·⁝·

One must know what contains and not become dispersed among the contents. What contains is above all the permanent miracle of existence, then the miracle of consciousness or intelligence, and then the miracle of joy, which—like an expansive and creative power—fills as it were the existential and intellectual "spaces".

———— ⫶ ————

What can a holy joy, a holy sadness, a holy passion, a holy anger be?

A disposition is holy to the extent that it draws us closer to God, which presupposes the quality of the subject as well as that of the object. Joy, for example, can be holy only on condition that it not be mingled with any fault of soul, and the object can be holy only if there be nothing in it which in fact does not draw us away from God.

But without having always to take into account the possible complexity of modalities, we shall say simply that the disposition of the soul is holy when its object or motivation is on the side of God, and when the soul is virtuous to the point of being in conformity with this object or motivation.

On the one hand, the heavenly object sanctifies the earthly subject; on the other hand, the virtuous subject sanctifies the earthly object, for this subject is heavenly in its turn.

—— ·⁝· ——

To be intelligent is to know how to distinguish between the essential and the secondary; but it is also
to intuit the essences or archetypes in phenomena. In
other words, intelligence may be either discriminat-
ing or contemplative, unless it be that discernment
and contemplation are in balance.

Discernment pertains more to the Absolute, and
contemplation more to the Infinite; we could also say
that will, or realization, pertains more to the Absoluteness of the Sovereign Good, while sentiment, or
love, pertains more to its Infinitude.

·⁝·

The mystery of certitude is that on the one hand, the
truth is inscribed in the very substance of our spirit
since we are "made in the image of God" and that
on the other hand, we are what we are able to know;
now we can know all that is, and That which alone is.

—— ·⁝· ——

Faith is peace of heart arising from an almost boundless certainty, which thus escapes by its very nature from the rights of doubt; human intelligence is made for transcendence, on pain of being no more than a multiplication of animal intelligence. Thus faith, apart from its completion by its content, is our disposition to know before knowing; even more, this disposition is already knowledge in that it derives from the innate wisdom which it is precisely the function of the revealed content of faith to reanimate.

The foundation of spiritual ascent is that God is pure Spirit and that man resembles Him fundamentally through the intelligence; man goes towards God by means of that which is, in him, most conformable to God—namely the intellect—which is at the same time both penetration and contemplation and has as its "supernaturally natural" content the Absolute which illumines and delivers.

—— ⫶ ——

Fundamentally there are only three miracles: existence, life, intelligence; with intelligence, the curve springing from God closes on itself like a ring that in reality has never been parted from the Infinite.

⫶

Intelligence, insofar as it belongs to us, is not sufficient unto itself, but has need of nobleness of soul, of piety and virtue, if it is to rise above its human particularity and be reunited with intelligence as such.

⫶

The intelligence of the animal is partial, that of man is total; and this totality is explained only by a transcendent reality to which the intelligence is proportioned.

———— ·:· ————

Objectivity, whereby human is distinguished from animal intelligence, would lack sufficient reason without the capacity to conceive the absolute or the infinite, or without the sense of perfection.

·:·

Objectivity is the essence of intelligence, but intelligence is often far from being conformed to its essence.

·:·

Intelligence is beautiful only when it does not destroy faith, and faith is beautiful only when it is not opposed to intelligence.

·:·

The fact that spiritual realism, or faith, pertains to the intelligence of the heart and not to that of the mind, permits one to understand that in spirituality, the moral qualification is more important than the intellectual qualification, and by far.

Among the qualities that are indispensable for spirituality in general: firstly, a mental attitude which for want of a better term could be designated by the word "objectivity": this is a perfectly disinterested attitude of the intelligence, and hence one that is free from ambition and prejudice and thereby accompanied by serenity. Secondly, we would mention a quality concerning the psychic life of the individual: this is nobility, or the capacity of the soul to rise above all things that are petty and mean; basically this is a discernment, in psychic mode, between the essential and the accidental, or between the real and the unreal. Finally, there is the virtue of simplicity: man is freed from every unconscious complex or compulsion stemming from self-love; he is free from pretension, ostentation, or dissimulation; in a word, he is without pride. Every spiritual method demands above all an attitude of poverty, humility, and simplicity or effacement, an attitude which is like an anticipation of Extinction in God.

—— ·⫶· ——

The synthesis and the substance of the moral qualities or of the virtues is Devotion: the integral attitude of man before God, made of reverential Fear and confident Love.

·⫶·

One cannot love God without fearing Him, any more than one can love one's neighbor without respecting him; not to fear God is to prevent Him from showing mercy.

·⫶·

Without fear of God as a basis, nothing is possible spiritually, for the absence of fear is a lack of self-knowledge.

·⫶·

To fear God is first of all to see, on the level of action, consequences in causes, sanction in sin, suffering in error; to love God is first to choose God, that is to say, to prefer what brings one nearer Him over what estranges from Him.

I am responsible, before God, for my soul; all else I leave in the hands of God. This means, firstly: I am not responsible for what others do; and secondly: I cannot change the world, or do away with every wrong, and I need not fret over this.

I am responsible, before God, for my soul, hence for my spiritual and social duties; I discriminate between what is essential and what is not, or between the real and the unreal. All else I leave in the hands of God: such are the virtues of resignation and trust.

⦙

It is readily said that God, or the divine Essence, is absolutely indefinable or ineffable; nevertheless, if one were to ask us which Name conveys the divine Essence, we would say that it is "the Holy", for holiness does not limit in any way, and it includes all that is divine; moreover, the notion of holiness transmits the perfume of the Divine as such, hence that of the Inexpressible.

Man is able to know, to will, to love. We know God in distinguishing Him from what is not He and in recognizing Him in what bears witness to Him; we will God in accomplishing what leads to Him and in abstaining from what removes from Him; and we love God in loving to know and to realize Him and in loving that which bears witness to Him, around us and within us.

·:·

Virtue is, in fact, the initial form of spiritual Union; without it, our knowing and our willing are of no use to us. Virtue—the deiformity of the feeling soul— makes fruitful both willing and knowing, it opens both faculties to Grace; it is thus that virtue is our "Life", that is, a readiness to receive and a presentiment of the Divine Life in us.

·:·

God being All that is, we must know Him, or love Him with all that we are; the quality of the Object calls forth that of the subject. "To know" God is to have as perfect an awareness of Him as possible; "to love" God is to tend towards Him in as perfect a manner as possible.

—— ⋅⎪⋅ ——

The gift of oneself to God is always the gift of oneself to all; to give oneself to God—though it were hidden from all—is to give oneself to man, for this gift of self has a sacrificial value of an incalculable radiance.

⋅⎪⋅

The consciousness of Being, or of the divine Substance, liberates us from narrowness, from agitation, from noise, and from pettiness; it is dilation, calm, silence, and grandeur. Every man in his innermost heart loves pure Being, the inviolable Substance, but this love is buried under a layer of ice. Every love is, in its depth, a tendency of the accident towards the Substance and for that very reason a desire for extinction.

⋅⎪⋅

"To extinguish oneself" or "to disappear" in the Will of God, is at the same time, and correlatively, to be at the disposition of the Divine Presence.

⋅⎪⋅

One can love man only as he should be loved, only in function of the Truth and of God.

———— ⁙ ————

Truth is the reason for man's existence; it constitutes our grandeur and reveals to us our littleness.

⁙

Even though we may be aware of certain qualities which are apparently our own, we are incapable of measuring ourselves with the measures of the Absolute. Whatever our worth, it is always nothing in comparison with the Divinity; we are therefore wasting our time mulling over nothingness. The only thing that has any meaning for us is the saving consciousness of the Absolute or, what humanly speaking comes to the same thing, the love of God.

⁙

There is no true greatness apart from truth.

⁙

If we want truth to live in us, we must live in it.

⁙

Truth is necessary for the perfection of virtue just as virtue is necessary for the perfection of truth.

———— ·⫶· ————

Every man loves to live in light and in fresh air; no one loves to be enclosed in a gloomy, airless tower. It is thus that one ought to love the virtues; and it is thus that one ought to hate the vices. No man who enjoys light or air would dream of saying: "I am the sun", or "I am the sky"; one loves the atmosphere of light and air, and that is why one enters into it. It is thus that one must enter into the virtues: because they impose themselves by their nature and because one loves their ambience.

·⫶·

A virtue is a divine perfume in which man forgets himself.

·⫶·

Truth and Holiness: all values are in these two terms; all that we must love and all that we must be.

·⫶·

There is no valid virtue without piety, and there is no authentic piety without virtue.

———— ∴ ————

Virtue is less the effort of acquiring qualities than the absence of faults; for, when evil is dissolved from within and combated from without, virtue shines forth; from the beginning it has slept within man, given that it stems from his deiformity.

∴

Virtue implies as much a sense of our littleness as it does a sense of the sacred.

∴

Poverty before God becomes richness before men: in other words, receptivity towards God becomes radiance and generosity towards men.

∴

Without generosity towards the world one cannot open oneself to Goodness and Mercy.

∴

The cosmic, or more particularly, the earthly function of beauty is to actualize in the intelligent creature the Platonic recollection of the archetypes, all the way into the luminous Night of the Infinite.

Beauty is a reflection of divine beatitude; and since God is Truth, the reflection of His beatitude will be that mixture of happiness and truth found in all beauty.

Sacred art helps man find his own center, that kernel whose nature is to love God.

The Sacred is an apparition of the Center, it immobilizes the soul and turns it towards the Inward.

·÷·

Hand in hand with the sense of the Divine goes the propensity to respect and the need to venerate; a predisposition which excludes profanity and triviality, and which is, therefore, opposed to all that is dispersion, ugliness, and noise. In creation all beauty is a door to the Sacred and a remembrance of God; an act of adoration.

⸻ ⋮ ⸻

The beauty of the sacred is a symbol or a foretaste of, and sometimes a means for, the joy that God alone procures.

⋮

The sacred is the presence of the center in the periphery, of the immutable in the moving; dignity is essentially an expression of it, for in dignity too the center manifests outwardly; the heart is revealed in gestures. The sacred introduces a quality of the absolute into relativities and confers on perishable things a texture of eternity.

⋮

The essential function of sacred art, apart from its simple didactic role, is to transfer Substance, which is both one and inexhaustible, into the world of accident and to bring the accidental consciousness back to Substance. One could say also that sacred art transposes Being to the world of existence, of action or of becoming, or that in a certain way it transposes the Infinite to the finite world, or Essence to the world of forms; it thereby suggests a continuity proceeding from the one to the other, a way starting from appearance or accident and issuing forth into Substance or into its celestial reverberations.

This lower world is an exile while being at the same time a reflection of Paradise.

·⫶·

There is, in the man who by nature is a "believer" or who "belongs to the elect", a legacy of the lost Paradise, and this is the instinct for the transcendent and the sense of the sacred; it is on the one hand the disposition to believe in the miraculous, and on the other hand the need to venerate and to worship. To this twofold predisposition must normally be added a twofold detachment, one in regard to the world and earthly life, and the other in regard to the ego, to its dreams and its pretensions.

·⫶·

Nature offers both vestiges of the earthly Paradise and foreshadowings of the heavenly Paradise.

·⫶·

Grace surrounds us infinitely, and it is only our hardness that makes us impervious to its radiation, which is in itself omnipresent; it is the soul that is absent, not grace.

———— ·⫶· ————

Doubtless, we may feel graces, but we may not base ourselves upon them. God will not ask us what we have experienced, but He will ask us what we have done.

·⫶·

When a man experiences a spiritual state or a grace, or if he has a vision or an audition, he must never desire that it be produced again, and above all, he must not base his spiritual life upon such a phenomenon nor imagine that it has conferred any eminence whatever upon him. The only thing that counts is to practice what brings us closer to God, while observing the conditions that this practice requires; we do not have God's measures, and we do not need to ask ourselves what we are. Life is a dream, and to think of God is to awaken; and it is to be in Heaven already here below.

Human life is studded with uncertainties; man loses himself in what is uncertain instead of holding on to what is absolutely certain in his destiny, namely death, Judgment, and Eternity. But besides these there is a fourth certainty, immediately accessible moreover to human experience, and this is the present moment, in which man is free to choose either the Real or the illusory, and thus to ascertain for himself the value of the three great eschatological certainties. The consciousness of the sage is founded upon these three points of reference, whether directly or in an indirect and implicit manner through "remembrance of God".

Paradise is there where God is. Hence remain next to God, and Paradise shall be there where you are.

There are two moments in life which are everything, and these are the present moment, when we are free to choose what we would be, and the moment of death when we have no longer any choice and when the decision belongs to God.

If the present moment is good, death will be good; if we are now with God—in this present which is ceaselessly being renewed but which remains always this one and only moment of actuality—God will be with us at the moment of our death.

The remembrance of God is a death in life; it will be a life in death.

·:·

The actualization of the consciousness of the Absolute—namely the "remembrance of God" or "prayer" insofar as it brings about a fundamental confrontation of creature and Creator—is already a death and a meeting with God and it places us already in Eternity; it is already something of Paradise and even, in its mysterious and "uncreated" quintessence, something of God. Quintessential prayer brings about an escape from the world and from life, and thereby confers a new and divine sap upon the veil of appearances and the current of forms, and a fresh meaning to our presence amid the play of phenomena.

Serenity is to keep oneself so to speak above the clouds, in the calm and coolness of emptiness and far from all the dissonances of this lower world; it is never to allow the soul to immerse itself in impasses of disturbances, bitterness, or secret revolt, for it is necessary to beware of implicitly accusing Being when accusing some phenomenon.

We would also say that serenity consists in resigning oneself to that destiny, at once unique and permanent, which is the present moment, to this itinerant "now" that no one can avoid and that in its substance pertains to the Eternal. The man who is conscious of the nature of pure Being willingly remains in the moment that Heaven has assigned him; he is not feverishly straining towards the future nor does he dwell lovingly or sadly over the past. The pure present is the moment of the Absolute: it is now—neither yesterday nor tomorrow—that we stand before God.

———— ·:· ————

It is correct to say that no one escapes his destiny; but it is right to add a conditional reservation, namely that fatality comprises different degrees, because our nature does so. Our destiny is dependent on the personal level—high or low—at which we halt or in which we enclose ourselves; for we are what we want to be and we undergo what we are.

·:·

Every injustice that we undergo at the hands of men is at the same time a trial that comes to us from God.

·:·

To accept a trial is to thank God for it, with the understanding that it permits us a victory: a detachment with relation to the world and with relation to the ego.

·:·

He is detached who never forgets the ephemeral nature of the things he possesses and who considers them loans, not possessions.

———— ·❘· ————

Even our own spirit does not belong to us, and we have full access to it only to the extent we know this.

·❘·

The sufficient reason for human intelligence is that of which it alone is capable: namely knowledge of the Sovereign Good, and in consequence all that refers to it directly or indirectly.

Similarly, the sufficient reason for the human will is that of which it alone is capable: namely the choice of the Sovereign Good and in consequence the practice of all that leads to it.

Similarly again, the sufficient reason for human love is that of which it alone is capable: namely love of the Sovereign Good and all that attests to it.

·❘·

Totality of intelligence implies freedom of will. This freedom would be meaningless without an end prefigured in the Absolute; without the knowledge of God and of our final ends, it would be neither possible nor useful.

———— ⋅⫶⋅ ————

The highest spiritual aptitude resides in man's capacity to surpass himself in view of God; this capacity is nothing without grace, but grace demands this capacity as nectar demands a vessel.

⋅⫶⋅

The human being, by his nature, is condemned to the supernatural.

⋅⫶⋅

The supreme Real concerns us in two ways: on the one hand it is the Immutable, which determines us, and on the other hand it is the Living, which attracts us.

⋅⫶⋅

To believe in God is to become again what we are; to become it to the very extent that we believe and that believing becomes being.

———— ⋮ ————

It is necessary to walk straight ahead on the crest of faith, and to say "yes" to the Sovereign Good which lights our way and which is the Goal.

⋮

It could be said that faith is that something which makes intellectual certitude become holiness; or which is the realizatory power of certitude.

⋮

Humanly, no one escapes the obligation to "believe in order to be able to understand".

⋮

The meaning and sufficient reason of man is to know, and to know is ineluctably to know the Divinity.

⋮

Spiritually speaking, to know oneself is to be conscious of one's limitations and to attribute every quality to God.

—— ·⁝· ——

Man deems himself good even before God, who is Perfection, and when he endeavors to recognize his wretchedness he again deems himself good on account of this effort.

·⁝·

Man cannot escape the duty of having to do good; it is in fact impossible under normal conditions not to do good; but what matters is that he knows it is God who acts. A meritorious work belongs to God, though we participate in it; our works are good—or better—to the extent we are penetrated by this awareness.

·⁝·

God likes to shatter and to renew forms or the husks of things; for He wants our hearts and is not content with our actions alone.

·⁝·

Only he is saved who trusts in God, and only he can have trust in God who is benevolent and generous.

—— ·⁝· ——

Nobility is made of elevation and compassion; by elevation it withdraws from things, and by compassion it comes back to them; but it comes back to them also by discernment and justice, for it is not made of charity alone, it is also made of resistance, given the nature of the world in which it has to manifest itself.

·⁝·

Nobility of character is beauty and grandeur of soul; it is therefore Virtue as such. And before having Virtue, one has to have the sense of Virtue, the love of moral beauty; a love which is efficacious to the extent that it is sincere.

·⁝·

The substance of human knowledge is Knowledge of the divine Substance.

·⁝·

Only the science of the Absolute gives meaning and discipline to the science of the relative.

———— ·⦙· ————

It is appropriate to distinguish equally between a knowledge that is active and mental, namely doctrinal discernment, by which we become conscious of the Truth, and a knowledge that is passive, receptive, and cardiac, namely invocatory contemplation, by which we assimilate what we have become aware of.

·⦙·

The soul is immortal because it is capable of knowing the Absolute; and it is capable of knowing the Absolute because it is immortal.

·⦙·

One of the proofs of our immortality is that the soul—which is essentially intelligence and consciousness—could not have an end that is beneath itself, namely matter or the mental reflections of matter; the higher cannot be merely a function of the lower, it cannot be merely a means in relation to what it surpasses. Thus it is intelligence in itself—and with it our freedom—which proves the divine scope of our nature and our destiny. Whether people understand it or not, the Absolute alone is "proportionate" to the essence of our intelligence.

Human intelligence is essentially objective, and thus total: it is capable of disinterested judgment, reasoning, assimilating and deifying meditation, with the help of grace. This character of objectivity also belongs to the will—it is this character that makes it human—and this is why our will is free, in other words capable of self-transcendence, sacrifice, and ascesis. Likewise for our soul, our sensibility and our capacity for loving: this capacity, being human, is by definition objective and thus disinterested in its essence or in its primordial and innocent perfection; it is capable of goodness, generosity, and compassion. It is from this specific nature, made of totality and objectivity, that the vocation of man, together with his rights and his duties, derives.

⋅⫶⋅

The habitual dream of ordinary man lives on the past and the future; his heart hangs, as it were, over the past and is carried away by the future at one and the same time, instead of resting in Being. God is Being in the absolute sense, He is Immutable and Omniscient; He loves what conforms to Being.

———— ·⦂· ————

Life is a dream, and to think of God is to awaken.

·⦂·

When man absents himself from the world for God, God makes Himself present in the world for man.

·⦂·

Be with God when times are easy, then, when times are difficult, God will be with you.

·⦂·

Life is not, as children and worldly people believe, a kind of space filled with possibilities offering themselves to our good pleasure; it is a road which becomes more and more narrow, from the present moment to death. At the end of this road there is death and the encounter with God, then eternity; now, all these realities are already present in prayer, in the timeless actuality of the divine Presence.

Man possesses a soul, and to have a soul means to pray. Like the soul itself, prayer comprises modes and each mode contains a virtue; to pray, then, is to actualize a virtue and at the same time to sow the seed of it. First of all comes resignation to the Will of God: acceptance of our destiny insofar as we cannot and should not change it; this attitude has to become second nature with us, given that there is always something from which we cannot escape. Correlative to this attitude or virtue there is the compensating attitude of trust: whoso puts his trust in God, while conforming to the Divine demands, will find God altogether disposed to come to his aid; but what we expect from Heaven we must ourselves offer to others: whoso desires mercy for himself must himself be merciful.

·|·

Every time man stands before God wholeheartedly—that is, "poor" and without being puffed up—he stands on the ground of absolute certitude, the certitude of his conditional salvation and the certitude of God. And that is why God has given us the gift of this supernatural key that is prayer: in order that we might stand before Him as in the primordial state, and as "always and everywhere"; or as in Eternity.

Orison, or quintessential prayer, implies an inward alternative, a choice between an imperfection arising from our nature and the remembrance of God, which is perfection. This alternative is above all an inner one, otherwise we would have no right to any outward act, and it is relative, otherwise we would have no right to any exclusive thought. Now quintessential prayer can superimpose itself on every licit act, and if it cannot do the same with regard to every useful or beautiful thought, it can at least continue to vibrate during such a thought.

·⫶·

Prayer—in the widest sense—triumphs over the four accidents of our existence: the world, life, the body, the soul; we might also say: space, time, matter, desire. It is situated in existence like a shelter, like an islet. In it alone we are perfectly ourselves because it puts us into the presence of God. It is like a diamond, which nothing can tarnish and nothing can resist.

·⫶·

If petition is a capital element of prayer, it is because we can do nothing without the help of God; man's resolves offer no guarantee if he does not ask for this help. It is not enough for a man to formulate his petition, he must express also his gratitude, resignation, regret, resolution, and praise.

The aim of individual prayer is not only to obtain particular favors, but also the purification of the soul: it loosens psychic knots or, in other words, dissolves subconscious coagulations and drains away many secret poisons; it externalizes before God the difficulties, failures, and tensions of the soul, which presupposes that the soul be humble and genuine, and this externalization—carried out in the face of the Absolute—has the virtue of reestablishing equilibrium and restoring peace, in a word, of opening us to grace.

·⫶·

Everything has already been said, and even well said; but it is always necessary to recall it anew, and in so doing, do what has always been done: to actualize in thought the certitudes contained, not in the thinking ego, but in the transpersonal substance of the human intelligence. Inasmuch as it is human, intelligence is total, hence essentially capable of the sense of the Absolute and correspondingly, of the sense of the relative; to conceive the Absolute is also to conceive the relative as such, and consequently to perceive in the Absolute the roots of the relative and, within the relative, the reflections of the Absolute.

———— ·⁙· ————

The only question that matters is our relationship with God.

One should never ask: "What is my worth?" nor: "Am I worthy of having a relationship with God?" For, in the first place, the question of our worth does not arise; the only thing that matters is our sincere relationship with God, outside of which there is no decisive human value. In the second place, the question of our dignity in relation to God does not arise either; being men, we are by definition "valid interlocutors" for God, and besides we have no choice; we are necessarily interlocutors, precisely because we belong to the human species.

And all of our relationships with the world depend upon our relationship with God. And it is this vertical relationship that authorizes, and even obliges us to trust: to place all of our cares in God's hands.

The Way is simple; it is man who is complicated.

One has to fight this complication of the soul, or the difficulties that the soul suffers or that it creates, in three ways.

Through the Intelligence: man becomes conscious of the relativity—and thereby of the nothingness—of things in function of the absoluteness of God.

Through the Will: man puts the Remembrance of God—thus consciousness of the Real—in place of the world, or of the ego, or of a given difficulty of the world or the ego.

Through Virtue: man escapes the ego and its miseries in withdrawing into his Center, in relation to which the ego is outward, as is the world.

These are the three perfections or the three norms. Perfection of intelligence; perfection of will; perfection of soul.

When the soul has recognized that its true being is beyond this phenomenal nucleus which is the empirical ego and when it willingly holds fast to the Center—and this is the chief virtue, poverty, or effacement, or humility—the ordinary ego appears to the soul as outward to itself, and the world, on the contrary, appears to it as its own prolongation; all the more so since it feels itself everywhere in the Hand of God.

———— ⁝ ————

God has opened a gate in the middle of creation, and this open gate of the world towards God is man; this opening is God's invitation to look towards Him, to tend towards Him, to persevere with regard to Him, and to return to Him. And this enables us to understand why the gate shuts at death when it has been scorned during life; for to be man means nothing other than to look beyond and to pass through the gate. Unbelief and paganism are whatever turns its back on the gate; on its threshold light and darkness separate. The notion of Hell becomes perfectly clear when we think how senseless it is—and what a waste and a suicide—to slip through the human state without being truly man, that is, to pass God by, and thus to pass our own souls by, as if we had any right to human faculties apart from the return to God, and as if there were any point in the miracle of the human state apart from the end which is prefigured in man himself; or again: as if God had had no motive in giving us an intelligence which discerns and a will which chooses.

Granted that this gate is a center—and it must be one since it leads to God—it corresponds to a rare and precious possibility, and one that is unique for its surroundings. And this explains why there is a damnation; for he who has refused to pass through the gate will never afterwards be able to cross its thresh-

—— ·∴· ——

old. Hence the representation of the afterlife as an implacable alternative: seen from the gate—that is, from the human state—there is no choice other than between the inside and the outside.

·∴·

What means everything for man is that the intelligence should become in fact, thanks to the content which corresponds to it, what it is in principle, and likewise, that the will should become really free thanks to the object which corresponds to it. In other terms: the intelligence is not truly intelligence except in so far as it discerns between the Real and the illusory, and the will is not truly free except in so far as it strives towards the Real.

———— ·⋮· ————

The prerogative of the human state is objectivity, whose quintessential content and ultimate reason for being is the Absolute. Objectivity of intelligence first of all; then objectivity of the will; and finally objectivity of the soul, of sensibility, of character, that is, objectivity both aesthetic and moral. The intelligence is objective to the extent that it registers that which is; the will is objective to the extent that it loves—by realizing it within itself—what is worthy of being loved.

The subject, whether it is intellective, volitive, or affective, seeks both the contingent and the Absolute; both the finite and the Infinite; both the imperfect and the Perfect. It seeks the contingent because it is itself contingent, and to the extent that it is so; and it seeks the Absolute because it grasps the Absolute by its capacity for objectivity, precisely.

Objectivity is a kind of death of the subject in the face of the reality of the object; the subjective compensation of this extinction is nobleness of character. One must not lose sight of the fact, moreover, that the transcendent Object is at the same time the immanent Subject, which is affirmed in the knowing subject, to the extent that the latter is capable of objectivity.

Objectivity is none other than the truth, in which the subject and the object coincide, and in which the essential takes precedence over the accidental—or in

—— ·⁝· ——

which the Principle takes precedence over its manifestation—either by extinguishing it, or by reinte-
grating it, according to the diverse ontological aspects
of relativity itself.

·⁝·

It has been said that man is a rational animal; while
this formulation is insufficient and ill-sounding, it
nonetheless points to an undeniable truth, though in
an elliptical fashion, for the rational faculty actually
serves to underscore the transcendence of man in relation to the animal. Man is rational because he possesses the Intellect, which by definition has a capacity
for the absolute and therefore a sense of the relative
as such; and he possesses the Intellect because he
is made "in the image of God", which he demon-
strates—it is hardly necessary to add—by his physical
form, his gift of speech, and his ability to produce
and construct. Man is a theophany in his form as well
as in his faculties.

·⁝·

Man finds his plenitude by placing himself in the
mold of the human Logos, whose intelligence, will,
and soul belong fully to God.

The foundation of the spiritual life and hence of the meaning of life as such is, on the one hand, Truth, hence the Certainty of the Supreme Real, which is the Sovereign Good, and on the other hand the Path, hence the Desire for Salvation, which is the supreme Happiness.

To these two imperatives there are necessarily joined two qualities or attitudes: Resignation to the Will of God and Trust in the Goodness of God.

These qualities in their turn imply two other virtues: Gratitude and Generosity.

Gratitude towards God is to appreciate the value of what God gives us and of what He has given us from our birth.

Gratitude towards man is to appreciate the value of what others give us, including surrounding nature; these gifts coincide ultimately with the gifts of God.

Generosity towards God—if one may say so—is to give ourselves to God, the quintessence of this gift being sincere and persevering orison.

Generosity towards man is to give ourselves to others, through charity in all its forms.

The two great basic virtues are humility and charity; in other words: self-knowledge and generosity towards others.

Self-knowledge: we do not say that one has to underestimate oneself and overestimate others; we say that one must not overestimate oneself nor underestimate others. Still, it is better to underestimate oneself and to overestimate others than to have the opposite attitude.

Generosity: we do not say that one has to grant favors to others which are contrary to their nature and which therefore they would abuse; we say that one has to grant them favors from which they may benefit without being tempted to abuse them. In other words: one must not heap favors upon others when they are not deserved, but one must grant others all possible extenuating circumstances materially and morally.

Generosity—or "charity"—is not weakness, any more than self-knowledge—or "humility"—is stupidity. This amounts to saying that virtue ought to conform to the nature of things; that it draws its nobleness and efficacy from truth. "There is no right superior to the right of truth"; and "beauty is the splendor of the true".

Poverty is being attached, in existence, neither to the subject nor to the object.

Much is said about subtle illusions and seductions which lead the spiritual pilgrim astray from the straight path and provoke his fall. Now, these illusions can only seduce him who desires some benefit for himself, such as powers or dignities or glory, or who desires inward joys or celestial visions or voices and so forth, or a tangible knowledge of divine mysteries.

But he who, in the orison, seeks nothing earthly, so that he is indifferent about being forgotten by the world, and who no longer seeks any sensation from the orison, so that he is indifferent about receiving anything sensible, such a man possesses true poverty and nothing can seduce him.

In true poverty, there remains only existence pure and simple, and existence is in its essence Being, Consciousness, and Beatitude. In poverty there remains nothing more for man than what he is, thus all that is.

The desire to vanquish faults because it is "I" who have them is ineffectual, since it falls within the same category as the faults themselves. Every fault, in fact, is a form of egoism or even of pride.

We must tend towards Perfection because we understand it and therefore love it, and not because we desire that our ego should be perfect. In other terms, we must love and realize a virtue because it is true and beautiful, and not because it would become us if we possessed it; and we must hate and fight against a fault because it is false and ugly, and not because it is ours and because it disfigures us. The nature of the effort must be determined by the object of the effort.

One must realize the virtues for their own sake, and not in order to make them "mine".

One may be sad because one displeases God, but not because one is not holy as others are.

To understand a virtue is to know how to realize it; to understand a fault is to know how to overcome it. To be sad because one does not know how to overcome a fault shows that one has not understood the nature of the corresponding virtue and that one's aspiration is motivated by egoism. Truth must be given precedence over self-interest.

To possess a virtue is first and foremost to be without the fault which is contrary to it, for God created us virtuous. He created us in His image; faults are superimposed. Moreover it is not we who possess virtue, it is virtue which possesses us.

It is less the pettinesses of the world that poison us than the fact of thinking of them too much.

We should never lose our awareness of the luminous and calm grandeur of the Sovereign Good, which dissolves all the knots of this world here below.

The fact that a particular phenomenon is lacking in beauty does not oblige us to lack in beauty ourselves; discernment is not mimicry. No doubt, we must take account of the dissonances of this world, but we must do so with an awareness of their proportions, which are always relative, and without losing contact with the serenity of Necessary Being. This, quite evidently, is in no way related to a false detachment which rests pridefully and hypocritically on errors and injustices, forgetting that "there is no right superior to that of the truth".

In spirituality more than in any other domain, it is important to understand that a person's character is a part of his intelligence: without a good character— one that is normal and consequently noble—intelligence, even if metaphysical, is largely ineffective. Our character is, first of all, what we will, and secondly, what we love; intelligence as such being what we know, or what we are capable of knowing. And knowledge of that which is outside us is of no avail without knowledge of ourselves.

That is why spiritual qualification implies moral qualification; will and sentiment being prolongations of the intelligence, which is essentially the faculty of adequation. Will, on the spiritual plane, is the disposition to realization; and sentiment—on the same plane—is the disposition to love what is objectively loveworthy: the true, the holy, the beautiful, the noble.

Beauty is a message that implies a reciprocity and a commitment: it implies a reciprocity between God and man, and a commitment from man to God.

In and by beauty, God gives us a message of His nature; He reveals for our sake an archetype and an essence. Beauty is a manifestation of Mercy, which pertains to Infinitude.

This gift of God requires a gift from man, a gift of self. Man, having glimpsed the Divine Beauty, has to show his gratitude by giving himself to God in his heart; to give oneself to God is the response proportionate to the earthly beauty in which God, in revealing Mercy, has given Himself to man.

·⋮·

For some, only the forgetting of the beautiful—of the "flesh", according to them—can bring us closer to God, which is obviously a valid point of view, at least in practice; for others—and this perspective is the more profound—sensible beauty too can bring us closer to God, on the twofold condition of a contemplativeness that apprehends the archetypes through the forms, and an interiorizing spiritual activity that eliminates the forms in view of the Essence.

—— ·⊹· ——

Beauty perceived outwardly must be discovered or realized inwardly, for we love that which we are and we are that which we love. Perceived beauty is not only the messenger of a heavenly and divine archetype, it is also, and for that very reason, the outward projection of a universal quality immanent in us, and quite obviously more real than our empirical and imperfect ego gropingly seeking its identity.

·⊹·

When we withdraw towards the heart, we will find therein all the beauties perceived outwardly; not as forms, but in their quintessential possibilities. In turning towards God, man can never lose anything.

·⊹·

When man interiorizes himself, God so to speak exteriorizes Himself while enriching man from within; there lies all the mystery of the metaphysical transparency of phenomena and of their immanence in us.

———— ⋅⋮⋅ ————

Auditive beauty is to visual beauty as essence is to form. Music is interiorized formal beauty as formal beauty is exteriorized music.

Similarly, mental beauty—poetry—is to corporeal beauty in action—dance—as essence is to form. Thus there is an affinity between mental beauty and auditive beauty—poetry and music—on the one hand, and between corporeal beauty in action and visual beauty—dance and beautiful forms—on the other hand.

The point here is the relationship between form and essence, or between manifestation and archetype, or between the outward and the inward. Outwardly perceived beauty must become, within us, archetypal and interiorizing music. We love that which we are in our essence, and we must be—or become—that which we love, and that which we have the right to love by the nature of things. This is the meaning of the beauties of the divine creation and of sacred art.

———— ·⊹· ————

The sacred is the projection of the celestial Center into the cosmic periphery, or of the "Motionless Mover" into the flux of things. To feel this concretely is to possess the sense of the sacred, and thereby the instinct of adoration, devotion, and submission; the sense of the sacred is the awareness—in the world of that which may or may not be—of That which cannot not be, and whose immense remoteness and miraculous proximity we experience at one and the same time. If we are able to have this awareness, it is because necessary Being reaches us in the depth of our heart, by a mystery of immanence which makes us capable of knowing all that is knowable, and which for that very reason makes us immortal.

·⊹·

The sense of beauty, actualized by a visual or auditive perception of the beautiful, or by a corporeal manifestation of beauty, whether static or dynamic, is equivalent to a "remembrance of God", provided it be in equilibrium with the "remembrance of God" properly speaking, which for its part requires the extinction of the perceptible. To the sensory perception of the beautiful, then, there must correspond a withdrawal towards the supra-sensible source of beauty; the perception of a sensible theophany demands unitive interiorization.

We are surrounded by a world of tumult and incertitude; and there are sudden encounters with things surprising, incomprehensible, absurd, or disappointing. But these things have no right to be problems for us, and this if only because every phenomenon has its causes, whether we know them or not.

Whatever may be the phenomena and whatever their causes, there is always That Which Is; and That Which Is, is beyond the world of tumult, contradictions, and disappointments. That Which Is can be troubled and diminished by nothing; It is Truth, Peace, and Beauty. Nothing can tarnish It, and no one can take It from us.

Whatever may be the din of the world or the soul, Truth will always be Truth, Peace will always be Peace, and Beauty will always be Beauty. These Realities are always tangible, they are always within our immediate reach; it suffices to look towards them and to steep ourselves in them. They are inherent in Existence itself; the accidents pass, the Substance remains.

Let the world be what it is and take refuge in Truth, Peace, and Beauty, wherein is neither doubt nor any blemish.

—— ·:· ——

There are people who torment themselves for even slight faults, committed even in the distant past, yet in the present they do what pleases God. Now it is a fault to reproach ourselves with what God does not reproach us.

God does not reproach us with a sin of which we are fully aware and which we have the sincere intention to commit no longer, if at the same time we practice what He requires and what brings us closer to Him.

Moreover, God does not ask us abstractly to be perfect, but asks us concretely not to have a particular fault and not to commit a particular sin or stupidity.

Furthermore, one must not ask oneself whether God asks this or that of us; if we accomplish what God certainly asks of us—namely prayer, invocation, the elementary virtues, and reasonable attitudes—we shall learn *ipso facto* what He may ask of us additionally.

God does not ask of us that of which we are unaware, any more than He reproaches us with what no longer exists.

God considers realities, not dreams. Objectivity is the key to every spiritual and moral value.

Man has the right not to accept an injustice—major or minor—from men, but he does not have the right not to accept it as a trial coming from God.

He has the right—for it is human—to suffer from an injustice insofar as he cannot rise above it, but he must make an effort to do so; in no case has he the right to plunge himself into a pit of bitterness, for such an attitude leads to hell.

Man has no interest, primarily, in overcoming an injustice; he has an interest primarily in saving his soul and in winning Heaven. Thus it would be a bad bargain to obtain justice at the price of our ultimate interests, to win on the side of the temporal and to lose on the side of the eternal, which is what man seriously risks when concern for his rights deteriorates his character or reinforces his faults.

When we encounter evil—and we owe it to God and to ourselves to maintain ourselves in Peace—we may utilize the following arguments. First of all, no evil can affect the Sovereign Good, nor should it trouble our relationship with God; upon contact with the absurd, we should never lose sight of absolute values. Secondly, we must be aware of the metaphysical necessity of evil. Thirdly, let us not lose sight of the limits and the relativity of evil; for *vincit omnia veritas.* Fourthly, it is obviously necessary to resign oneself to the will of God, that is, to our destiny; destiny, by definition, is what we cannot escape. Fifthly— and this follows from the preceding argument—God wills to try our faith, hence also our sincerity, our trust, and our patience; and that is why one speaks of the "trials of life". Sixthly, God will not ask us to account for what others do, nor for what happens to us when we are not responsible for it; He asks us to account for what we ourselves have done. Seventhly, and finally, happiness is not for this life, but for the next; perfection is not of this world, and the last word belongs to Beatitude.

———— ⫶ ————

Life in human society favors the appearance of social vices, but this is not a reason for not resisting them, quite to the contrary. Victory over the vices is owed to the men around us as well as to God who observes us and who will judge us.

First of all there is pride: it is to overestimate oneself while underestimating others; it is the refusal to accept humiliation when the nature of things requires it; and it is *ipso facto* to take for a humiliation every attitude that simply reveals our limits.

Next there is egoism: it is to think only of one's own interest and thus to forget that of others. It is in this sector that egocentrism and narcissism are situated, without forgetting touchiness.

Stupidity is the lack of discernment between the essential and the secondary and, as a result, that moral ugliness which is pettiness; it is also the lack of sense of proportions, hence of priorities.

Wickedness is the will to harm another, in one fashion or other; it is especially slander, calumny, and spite.

Hypocrisy consists in practicing all the vices while practicing spiritual exercises, which in this context become sacrileges.

———— ⫶ ————

The two great pitfalls of earthly life are outwardness and matter; or more exactly disproportionate
outwardness and corruptible matter. Outwardness is
the lack of balance between our tendency towards
outer things and our tendency towards the inward;
and matter is the lower substance—lower in relation
to our spiritual nature—in which we are imprisoned
on earth. In Heaven, our matter will be transubstanti-
ated.

What is called for is, not to reject the outward
while allowing only the inward, but to realize a relationship with the inward—a spiritual inwardness
precisely—that removes from outwardness its dis-
persing and compressing tyranny, and that allows
us to "see God everywhere"; that is, to perceive in
things symbols and archetypes, in short, to integrate
the outward in the inward and to make the outward
a support for inwardness. Beauty perceived by a spiritually interiorized soul is interiorizing. One must not
confuse a proud or narcissistic inwardness with holy
inwardness.

And as regards matter: the point is not to deny
it—as if that were possible—but to remove oneself
from its seductive tyranny; to distinguish in it the archetypal and pure from the accidental and impure; to
treat it with nobility and sobriety. "For the pure all
things are pure."

———— ·.·. ————

Man is subject to two poles of attraction, that of the outward world and that of the inward center. Drawn towards the outward, he is plunged in concupiscence and anxiety; drawn towards the inward, he finds certitude and peace.

For man, outwardness is a right, and inwardness a duty. We have the right to outwardness in the measure that we are men, or because we are men; and we must realize inwardness—hence live towards the inward—because our spiritual substance is not of this world; neither, in consequence, is our destiny.

The outward is the dimension of accidents; the inward, that of substance. Or to put it differently: the outward is the dimension of forms; the inward, that of the essence.

When man has achieved a balance between the inward and the outward, the outward is no longer equated with concupiscence and anxiety; it is in a certain way interiorized, its contents are transparent. This is to see the substance in the accidents, or the essence in the forms.

When we withdraw into the inward, the inward by compensation will manifest itself to us in the outward. Nobleness of soul is to have a sense of the archetypes.

Being alone with God: rightness of Intention requires that there not be any false note in this desire for holy solitude. One cannot want to be alone with God because one scorns men—this would amount to saying that God alone is good enough for us and that we do not belong to mankind—nor because one overestimates oneself, precisely. There must be in this holy desire neither bitterness nor pride; the soul that isolates itself before God must have a feeling of goodwill and respect towards its fellows, it must not have any feeling of personal superiority or of resentment. However, man has perfectly the right to know that the world is bad—the world and not all men—and he cannot even be prevented from having this awareness; it is a part of Discernment. But he is not alone in having this awareness, nor alone in loving God; nor alone in being loved by God, above all.

There is an outer man and an inner man; the first lives in the world and undergoes its influence, whereas the second looks towards God and lives from the orison. Now it is necessary that the outer man not affirm himself to the detriment of the inner man; it is the inverse which must take place. Instead of inflating the outer man and allowing the inner man to die, it is necessary to allow the inner man to expand, and to entrust the cares of the outer to God.

Who says outer man says preoccupations of the world, or even worldliness: in effect there is in every man a tendency to attach himself too much to this or that element of passing life or to worry about it too much, and the adversary takes advantage of this in order to cause troubles for us. There is also the desire to be happier than one is, or the desire not to suffer any injustices, even harmless ones, or the desire always to understand everything, or the desire never to be disappointed; all of this is of the domain of subtle worldliness, which must be countered by serene detachment, by the principial and initial certainty of That which alone matters, then by patience and trust. When no help comes from Heaven, this is because it is a question of a difficulty which we can and must resolve with the means which Heaven has placed at our disposal. In an absolute way, it is necessary to find our happiness in the orison; that is to say that it is necessary to find therein sufficient happiness so as not to allow ourselves to be excessively troubled by the things of the world, seeing that dissonances cannot but exist, the world being what it is.

There is the desire not to suffer any injustices, or even simply not to be placed at a disadvantage. Now one of two things: either the injustices are the result of our past faults, and in this case our trials exhaust this causal mass; or the injustices result from our character, and in this case our trials bear witness to it; in both cases, we must thank God and invoke Him with all the more fervor, without preoccupying ourselves with worldly chaff. One must also say to oneself that the grace of the orison compensates infinitely for every dissonance from which we can suffer, and that in relation to this grace, the inequality of terrestrial favors is a pure nothingness. Let us never forget that an infinite grace compels us to an infinite gratitude, and that the first stage of gratitude is the sense of proportions.

The first criterion of spirituality is that a man manifest his consciousness of the incommensurability between the Real and the illusory, the Absolute and the relative, God and the world.

The second criterion is that a man manifest his choice of the Real: that he understand the imperious necessity for active attachment to the Real; for a concrete, operative, and saving relationship with God.

The third criterion is that, knowing that the Real is the Sovereign Good and that consequently It contains and projects all beauty, a man conform himself to It with all his soul; for that which he knows to be perfect, and that which he wishes to attain, that he must also be, and that he is through the virtues, and not otherwise.

Man possesses an intelligence, a will, and a soul: a capacity for understanding, a capacity for willing, and a capacity for loving. Each of these three faculties comprises an essential and supreme function which is its reason for being, and lacking which we would not be human beings; a function determined by the Real and contributing to salvation. Total knowledge, free will, and disinterested love; intelligence capable of absoluteness, will capable of sacrifice, soul capable of generosity.

All the dogmas, all the prescriptions, and all the means of a religion have their sufficient reason in the

———— ·ǀ· ————

three fundamental vocations of man: in discernment, in practice, and in virtue.

And man bears within himself all the gifts and means of a religion, but he no longer has access to them on account of the fall; whence precisely the necessity—relative, in principle—of outward forms that awaken and actualize man's spiritual potentialities.

The "High" accepts the homage of the "low" only on condition that, on the plane of the "low", the "left" render homage to the "right". In other words, God accepts man's homage only on condition that the inferior man render homage to the superior man; the integrity of the vertical relationship demands that of the horizontal relationship. Therein lies the principle of all human order; for to say human is to say hierarchy. A man is superior to the extent that he represents God, or inasmuch as he represents Him—as does the prophet, the saint, the spiritual authority, the monarch, the priest, or simply the man who is better than we are, and in the particular respect that this is so. It is in any case impossible to have a salvific relationship with God when one underestimates, or even holds in contempt, men who are at the least worthy of respect.

The world, life, and human existence show themselves to be in practice a complex hierarchy of certainties and uncertainties. To the question of what are the foremost things a man should do, situated as he is in this world of enigmas and fluctuations, the reply must be made that there are four things to be done or four jewels never to be lost sight of: firstly, he should accept the Truth; secondly, bear it continually in mind; thirdly, avoid whatever is contrary to Truth and the permanent consciousness of Truth; and fourthly, accomplish whatever is in conformity therewith. All religion and all wisdom is reducible, extrinsically and from the human standpoint, to these four laws: enshrined in every tradition is to be observed an immutable truth, then a law of "attachment to the Real", of "remembrance" or "love" of God, and finally prohibitions and injunctions; and these make up a fabric of elementary certainties which encompasses and resolves human uncertainty, and thus reduces the whole problem of earthly existence to a geometry that is at once simple and primordial.

———— ·⫶· ————

The essential function of human intelligence is discernment between the Real and the illusory or between the Permanent and the impermanent, and the essential function of the will is attachment to the Permanent or the Real. This discernment and this attachment are the quintessence of all spirituality; carried to their highest level or reduced to their purest substance, they constitute the underlying universality in every great spiritual patrimony of humanity, or what may be called the *religio perennis*; this is the religion to which the sages adhere, one which is always and necessarily founded upon formal elements of divine institution.

·⫶·

The human vocation is to realize that which is man's reason for being: a projection of God and, therefore, a bridge between Earth and Heaven; or a point of view that allows God to see Himself starting from an other-than-Himself, even though this other, in the final analysis, can only be Himself, for God is known only through God.

The notion of the Absolute and the love of God are without beginning and without end, and it is by these or because of these that man possesses immortality; that is to say the notion of the Absolute and the love of God constitute the very essence of human subjectivity—this subjectivity which is a proof both of our immortality and of God, and which is, properly speaking, a theophany.

The immortal soul did not begin at birth; it is the divine spirit that God breathed into man at the time of creation. That is why man, to the extent that he conforms to his nature and thus to his vocation, is without beginning, hence "uncreated", as some have said. There lies the metaphysical meaning of this saying: "And no man hath ascended up to heaven, but he that came down from heaven."

The notion of the Absolute and the love of God are Eternal.

∴

It is not we who know God, it is God who knows Himself in us.

What is the world if not a flow of forms, and what is life if not a cup which seemingly is emptied between one night and another? And what is prayer, if not the sole stable point—a point of peace and light—in this dream universe, and the strait gate leading to all that the world and life have sought in vain? In the life of a man, these four certitudes are all: the present moment, death, the meeting with God, eternity. Death is an exit, a world which closes down; the meeting with God is like an opening towards a fulgurating and immutable infinitude; eternity is a fullness of being in pure light; and the present moment is, in our duration, an almost ungraspable "place" where we are already eternal—a drop of eternity amid the to and fro of forms and melodies. Prayer gives to the terrestrial instant its full weight of eternity and its divine value; it is the sacred ship bearing its load, through life and death, towards the further shore, towards the silence of light—but at bottom it is not prayer which traverses time as it repeats itself, it is time which, so to speak, halts before the already celestial unicity of prayer.

The world is made up of forms, and they are as it were the debris of a celestial music that has become frozen; knowledge or sanctity dissolves our frozen state and liberates the inner melody.

·:·

Man prays, and prayer fashions man. The saint has himself become prayer, the meeting place of earth and Heaven; he thereby contains the universe, and the universe prays with him. He is everywhere where nature prays, and he prays with her and in her: in the peaks, which touch the void and eternity; in a flower, which scatters its scent; in the carefree song of a bird.

He who lives in prayer has not lived in vain.

APPENDIX

Selections from Letters
and Other Unpublished Writings

The peace of man is nothing, for it is based on the belief that suffering is an accident from which one can escape. Men are strong and self-assured because they are ignorant; but ignorance cannot be a virtue. Were they able to see, they would tremble and be faint-hearted, and that would be better. It is better to see and be weak, than to be blind and strong, for seeing may well lead to strength, but blindness only to suffering.

·:·

For the ignorant man, the world is like measureless space, filled with unrestricted possibilities; for him, God is like a fixed point. For the spiritual man, the world is like a point, which has only one possibility; for him, the Divine is like measureless space, in which he loses himself in primordial free flight and is extinguished, like a star as morning approaches.

What is the primordial doctrine? It is the knowledge of ultimate relationships, enveloped in forms, manifesting itself in forms, continually returning in fresh shapes throughout human ages and yet remaining eternally the same. This Truth, living in multiple forms, limited by none, always leading back to the pure Spirit, is the primordial doctrine.

It is the product of no human thinking. It belongs to no one. He who knows it, possesses it; but in truth, it embraces him and has absorbed the knower into itself—It, the Eternal, has absorbed him who is ephemeral. Thus does the sea absorb a drop. Its entrance is everywhere and nowhere. It is without origin and without end.

·:·

God is the Good, and only He is the Good as such—the Good in an absolute way.

Extrinsically speaking, this Good is always here and always now, because we—who are in relativity—are always here and now; because our very being is in space and time. Say creature, and you say here and now.

And as God is intrinsically the source of our happiness, we should be happy everywhere and at any time; we should not forget it in the early morning, when we remember what we are and who we are.

Wisdom cannot bear fruit in a soul without virtues, for the object of Wisdom is God, and God is virtuous. God is virtuous, not because virtues limit Him, which is impossible, but because there is no virtue which does not derive from Him, and which does not exist in Him in an infinite manner. The fundamental divine virtue is Beauty; it explains everything. It is from it that are derived Goodness and Strength, Mercy and Justice, Love and Will. As for Wisdom, it is not a virtue, it is Being itself: God being wise in Himself, He is wise in each virtue; there is no virtue which excludes His Wisdom. Justice excludes Mercy—not in an absolute fashion, but in a certain respect—while neither Justice nor Mercy exclude Wisdom, any more than they exclude Sanctity or Infinity.

Metaphysical wisdom is certainly independent of human virtues, but the man who wishes to realize this wisdom is not independent of the virtues, since it is through them that he participates humanly in the Truth.

———— ⫶ ————

Our existence has no other meaning than prayer, this perpetual gazing at God. God knows that we are weak, and does not expect miracles from us; but the little that we can do for the next world can be infinitely meaningful.

If God demands of us that we do something outwardly "useful", we can discover this only on the basis of our unconditional surrender to the orison; for it never happens that a man errs in thinking of God.

⫶

In the face of God, we creatures have no measure for our virtues; at the Last Judgment we shall lay before God like a flat surface; then He, the Absolute, will have mercy on some creatures. We may, in our fashion, be "good", but we cannot measure this "goodness" of ours against the Absolute. If it were otherwise, the Absolute would not be absolute, and God would not be God.

You ask me what one must do to overcome bad habits. First of all, one needs to be aware of their causes and also of their consequences; one must objectivize them, see them for what they are and know where they lead us to. One needs to know in what way they are opposed to the fundamental virtues of purity, strength, peace, and fervor, and to the attitudes of knowledge and union. A fault is always opposed to one of these.

Hindus say that nothing can resist knowledge, that "there is no lustral water equal to it". This is because it is easy to become detached from something that one has objectivized perfectly, that is to say from something that one is able to see from high above. It is difficult to become detached from something with which one is identified.

Next, one must pray that God help us. One must describe our state and our difficulties to God.

Apart from our individual problems, the orison helps us and transforms us. One must therefore pray much, by forgetting who we are and by investing all of our life and all of our being into the orison, something which moreover is in keeping with the Supreme Commandment, that of the perfect love of God.

Firstly, we must find our joy in God, not in the world; it follows from this that we must not be disappointed if we do not find our joy in the world.

Secondly, we must surrender ourselves to God, and judge the world from the standpoint of this surrender. We must not let the absurdity of the world sap our blood so that we are turned away from our surrender to God.

Thirdly, we must not forget that the evil enemy provokes absurdity in order to bewilder us and turn us away from God. Our surrender may not, cannot, depend on our understanding all riddles; it is unconditional, depending only on the Truth of truths. Surrender to God was there before the existence of the world, and before we ourselves existed; we do not create it, we enter into it; it is our deep, eternal Being.

Our trust in God must protect us from doubts about the world; it must be stronger than all absurdity. Otherwise it would be as if we had doubts about the Truth of truths, whereas in fact this Truth is our real Being.

Outer man is so made that he always waits for joys coming from the outside and has difficulty accepting that joy lies in the inner man; thus it may happen that a sadness not directly connected to the vicissitudes of his surroundings may befall the outer man. The spiritual wanderer lives between two worlds; the earth is no more his homeland, and Heaven not yet, or at least so it seems.

Man—I mean the simply worldly man, not the spiritual and specially blessed man—is mostly not at all with himself, he passes himself and his happiness by; for most people life is a sort of betrayal, and they almost never come to themselves; everything is flight and alienness. But one must arrive far enough—and with God's Grace it is possible—so as to rediscover the happy, innocent moment and then never to lose it again; it is the pure, golden, vernal grace of the Origin and of spiritual childhood.

———— ⸪ ————

Faith—that is everything! Most men suffer from the fact that they have too little faith in one respect or another. In a certain sense, lack of faith is a lack of imagination; one is too locked up in one's little earthly dream and cannot correctly gauge the tremendous grace of the orison; one cannot place oneself from the point of view of the hereafter, from whence everything earthly seems distant and small—except for the orison! We should dance for joy and gratitude that destiny brought us the gift of this grace; everything else is but a dream. It is precisely the fate of earthly life that we see what is small in front of us as being immense and that what is great appears to us as small. And one is lacking in faith also because one loses sight of the truth. In one fashion or another, one underestimates God's goodness, that is why one lacks trust. Knowledge of the nothingness of the world; then of the orison within us; and then patience and trust; that is everything!

The relative cannot withstand the Absolute. Outer and inner difficulties are relative; the orison is absolute. Hence: perseverance is everything! And blessed the man who has overcome the trial.

The question to be asked is not whether we are good or bad, healthy or ill, gifted or ungifted, but simply whether or not we acknowledge God, cease doing stupid things, and invoke God's Name. If yes, then all is won, whatever our outward life may be.

·:·

Natural nobility has no effective value except to the extent that it is integrated into supernatural virtue; natural nobility does not exclude pride, only supernatural nobility excludes it, so that it could be said that supernatural nobility coincides with humility; where humility is, there also is charity. The reflex of self-defense and the tendency to suspicion are serious obstacles; a humble man is ready to accept even an exaggerated criticism if it comprises a grain of truth and if it emanates from an honorable man. A humble man has no interest in having his nobility recognized, he is interested only in rising above himself, hence in pleasing God more than men.

People speak of a duty to make oneself useful to society, but they omit to ask the question whether that society does or does not in itself possess the usefulness that a human society normally should exhibit, for if the individual must be useful to the collectivity, the latter for its part must be useful to the individual, and one must never lose sight of the fact that there exists no higher usefulness than that which envisages the final ends of man. By its divorce from traditional truth—as primarily perceivable in that "flowering forth" which is revelation—society forfeits its own justification, doubtless not in a perfunctorily animal sense, but in the human sense. This human quality implies that the collectivity, as such, cannot be the aim and purpose of the individual but that, on the contrary, it is the individual who, in his "solitary stand" before the Absolute and in the exercise of his supreme function, is the aim and purpose of the collectivity. Man, whether he be conceived in the plural or the singular, or whether his function be direct or indirect, stands like "a fragment of absoluteness" and is made for the Absolute; he has no other choice before him. In any case, one can define the social in terms of truth, but one cannot define truth in terms of the social.

———— ·:· ————

Concentration depends on our awareness of the motives. What is lacking in many—but this is quite human—is the sense of the concrete on the spiritual plane; and the sense of the concrete, it must be said, is something altogether different from the sense of the sublime; the first has its demands whereas the second costs nothing. It is all good and well to have doctrinal knowledge, but one must also have faith; and faith is a kind of mystery. It is, moreover, largely a question of imagination: one must transfer imaginativeness into the domain of the "one thing needful". The human soul is like an opaque and ponderous mountain that obstructs the way toward immanent Beatitude; but in reality it is but a mist. *Vincit omnia Veritas.*

In many cases, the ill-sounding remarks of one person have been provoked by the affirmations of another, and one often fails to take these latter into account; it also happens that the remarks which one criticizes are isolated from their indispensable context; sometimes people unconsciously falsify things which they recount; one must never lose sight, moreover, of the fact that many people do not know how to express themselves adequately, above all in a conversation, for the precise expression of thought is an art which requires a certain mental discipline. Be that as it may, instead of silently recording a remark which astonishes one or scandalizes one, one should immediately ask questions and ask for exact details, in one's own interest as well as in that of the interlocutor. When someone reports that he heard someone express an opinion which seems to be false, one should immediately ask: "And what did you answer?" or "what explanation were you given?" Otherwise, the person who reports the comment is gravely culpable, possibly as much or even more so than the person he accuses and to whom he has not furnished the occasion to explain himself.

There are persons who relate ill-sounding comments and who have done nothing to settle the question with the interlocutor; this is neither logical nor moral. If one has forgotten to do so, or if one has not had the presence of mind or the courage to do so, then one should simply forget the incident as well!

Every man is in search of happiness; this is another dimension of human nature. Now there is no perfect happiness outside God; any earthly happiness has need of Heaven's blessing. Prayer places us in the presence of God, who is pure Beatitude; if we are aware of this, we will find Peace in it. Happy the man who has the sense of the Sacred and who thus opens his heart to this mystery.

The beginning of perfection is objectivity with regard to oneself and indifference with regard to the question of our actual worth; the spiritual man is not interested in the question of knowing if he is perfect or not, he simply wants to vanquish his imperfections, not in order to be able to feel perfect, but because his imperfections are false. His obligatory point of departure is the idea that he is imperfect; no spiritual man is either astonished or desperate when one tells him this; his disposition to admit it is even a fundamental criterion of his spirituality.

That which is "absoluteness" in God is "perfection" in the Envoy of God. How can one describe this? First of all, of course, it means being free from psychic and physical vices; these are above all pride, ambition, pettiness, maliciousness, which are never to be found in the perfect man. But then I would say—and this may sound surprising: the perfect man is the man who loves God and who is able to think; and since he is able to think, he also loves his neighbor—not blindly, but according to the data of Reality; for since one cannot love oneself measurelessly as an earthly phenomenon, one may also not love one's neighbor measurelessly; now with respect to God there is no longer any measure.

Once again: what does it mean to link perfection with the capacity to think? It means this: all too many people are considered "intelligent" because they are excellent at thinking as long as their thinking moves in the grooves of their sentimental wishes and prejudices. As soon as this is no longer the case, they cannot think any more; I do not call such people "intelligent", be they brilliant philosophers. This is why I wrote somewhere, "To be objective is to die a little." By all this I mean: what one should note in the perfect man—apart from the absence of vices—is above all the capacity to think quite independently of possible feelings or wishes. To ascribe to such a man sentimental or interested prejudices is the surest sign of a deep-lying imperfection; for the inferior man—however gifted he may be—transfers in his imagination his own inferiorities into the soul of the other, he sees the other as he should see himself—which, precisely, he is not capable of doing. This incapacity is precisely the touchstone of his inferiority. In certain cases this psychophysical lack is curable, in others not; it is curable if it is superficial, thus due to outer circumstances, but not if it lies in the soul's substance. But I must add here that there is nothing absolute in the world—God alone is absolute—and that in God and through God things are possible which appear impossible to man.

Now he who really loves God can also think; for the love of God—the Knowledge of God—admits no limitations that would affect thinking. The incapacity to think always accords with pride; for the truly humble man is always inclined to look at himself from outside and from above; he wants to belong to God, not to himself!

What We Should Teach Our Children

There is one God, who is in Heaven; who is good and powerful; who created the World and everything in it; to whom we will go if we are good, and who will punish us if we are bad; to whom we must pray every day, in the morning, between noon and afternoon, and in the evening.

One should not allow oneself to take the dissonances of life too much to heart, for happiness is to be found less in what we experience in time than in what lies before us in Eternity and which no one can take away from us. Every believer knows this, yet it is easily forgotten in the maelstrom of life. Imagine a man living in the poor quarter of a city; he would like to have a beautiful home in the rich quarter; he frets over all sorts of details, while all along he carries with him a golden key that after a while will enable him to enter the Eternal Jerusalem; only he has the key, the rich of the earthly city do not have it, and the city will in any case perish. Now, I ask: is not happiness to be found in your possession of the key, wherever we may be?

It may happen that a person who accepts justified criticisms does not accept a criticism if it is not *a priori* understandable to him.

In fact, nobody accepts a criticism which seems not to be justified.

A person who stubbornly does not accept criticisms is a person who refuses to accept a criticism whose justification has been proven and fully explained. But the proofs must be founded on reality and not merely on logical appearance!

There are sentimental people who believe that any criticism, even if it is entirely false, must be accepted for mystical reasons, but this has nothing to do either with truth or with justice.

The question is not whether we accept a criticism or not, the question is why we do not accept it.

Even if a man is wrong in some cases, this does not mean that he is always wrong. Even if a man is right in some cases, this does not mean that he is always right.

It is better to accept an unjustified criticism than to refuse a justified one; I am talking of exceptions, not of rules. I say that the acceptance of a minor injustice is a lesser evil; I do not say that it is a good thing in itself.

―――― ·⫶· ――――

We say that there is an absolute, transcendent Reality, unperceivable by the senses, beyond space and time; but knowable by the pure Intellect, by which It makes Itself present; a Reality which, without ever undergoing the least change since It is unconditional, gives rise—by virtue of Its very Infinitude—to a dimension of contingency or relativity in order to be able to realize the mystery of Its radiation. For "it is in the nature of the Good to wish to communicate Itself": this means that God wishes to be known not only in Himself, but also "from without" and starting from an "other than He"; that is the very substance of the Divine All-Possibility.

This is what we say, or recall, *a priori*. We say it, not only because we believe it, but because we know it, and we know it because we are it. We are it in our transpersonal Intellect, which intrinsically is the vehicle of the immanent Presence of the Absolute Real, and without which we would not be men.

———— ·⋮· ————

How can the spiritual man conquer the natural tendency to sadness that old age entails? It will be said: by the hope of a better hereafter; but this is not enough, for the elderly person must find already in the here-below a reason to be happy, and it is Faith. Faith is our relationship with God; if this relationship is living, then the possibility of dominating our purely natural tendencies is already there.

Man lives in time; God is the Eternal. In prayer, the human and the Divine meet—when we say "Yes" to God in the depths of our heart.

EDITOR'S NOTES

3: *From the Divine to the Human* (Bloomington, IN: World Wisdom, 1982), "To Refuse or To Accept Revelation".

Logic and Transcendence (Bloomington, IN: World Wisdom, 2009), "Concerning the Proofs of God".

Stations of Wisdom (Bloomington, IN: World Wisdom, 1995), "The Stations of Wisdom".

Survey of Metaphysics and Esoterism (Bloomington, IN: World Wisdom, 1985), "Substance: Subject and Object".

4: *Esoterism as Principle and as Way* (Bedfont: Perennial Books, 1981), "Dimensions of the Human Vocation".

Light on the Ancient Worlds (Bloomington, IN: World Wisdom, 2006), "*Religio Perennis*".

5: *From the Divine to the Human*, "To Refuse or To Accept Revelation".

Esoterism as Principle and as Way, "The Problem of Sexuality".

The Book of Keys, "On the Two Themes".

Roots of the Human Condition (Bloomington, IN: World Wisdom, 1991), "On Love".

6: *The Book of Keys*, "The Way".

"Caractères de la Mystique Passionnelle", in *Études Traditionnelles*, July-August and September, 1953. Schuon later revised this article and included it in *The Transfiguration of Man* (Bloomington, IN: World Wisdom, 1995) under the title "Characteristics of Voluntaristic Mysticism". This passage however was not included in the final English version of the article.

7: *Survey of Metaphysics and Esoterism*, "Substance: Subject and Object".

The Book of Keys, "Being Happy".

Logic and Transcendence, "Concerning the Love of God".

8: *The Book of Keys*, "Substance and Accidents".

Logic and Transcendence, "Man and Certainty".

9: *The Book of Keys*, "Al-Mahabbah".

Stations of Wisdom, "The Stations of Wisdom".

The Book of Keys, "Love of God".

In the Face of the Absolute (Bloomington, IN: World Wisdom, 1989), "The Mystery of the Prophetic Substance".

10: *From the Divine to the Human*, "To Refuse or To Accept Revelation".

Stations of Wisdom, "Orthodoxy and Intellectuality".

The Transcendent Unity of Religions (Wheaton, IL: Quest, 1984), "To Be Man Is To Know".

Sufism: Veil and Quintessence (Bloomington, IN: World Wisdom, 2006), "Tracing the Notion of Philosophy".

11: *Esoterism as Principle and as Way*, "The Degrees of Art".

Esoterism as Principle and as Way, "Foundations of an Integral Aesthetics".

12: *The Book of Keys*, "Recapitulation of the Doctrine".

Survey of Metaphysics and Esoterism, "Trials and Happiness".

Esoterism as Principle and as Way, "Dimensions of the Human Vocation".

13: *The Book of Keys*, "On Holiness".

———— ⫶ ————

The Book of Keys, "I and Things".

The Book of Keys, "*Hikmah Maryamīyah*".

14: *Spiritual Perspectives and Human Facts* (Bloomington, IN: World Wisdom, 2007), "Thought and Civilization".

To Have a Center (Bloomington, IN: World Wisdom, 1990), "The Primacy of Intellection".

Letter of 14 February 1983.

15: *The Book of Keys*, "The Reciprocal Yes".

Light on the Ancient Worlds, "Man in the Universe".

The Book of Keys, "Faith Is To Say 'Yes'".

The Book of Keys, "Faith Is To Say 'Yes'".

16: *From the Divine to the Human*, "The Sense of the Sacred".

From the Divine to the Human, "To Refuse or To Accept Revelation".

The Book of Keys, "Truth and Faith, Work and Virtue".

The Book of Keys, "The Heart Is the Themes".

—— ·:· ——

The Book of Keys, "Combating the Faults of the Soul".

17: *Roots of the Human Condition*, "Virtue and Way".

The Book of Keys, "The Six Fundamental Givens".

Esoterism as Principle and as Way, "The Triple Nature of Man".

18: *The Book of Keys*, "The Sinner Saved".

Stations of Wisdom, "Complexity of the Concept of Charity".

19: *Stations of Wisdom*, "Complexity of the Concept of Charity".

Personal notebook, 1953.

Esoterism as Principle and as Way, "Foundations of an Integral Aesthetics".

The Book of Keys, "To Understand, To Love, To Practice".

20: *The Book of Keys*, "Anonymity of the Virtues".

The Book of Keys, "The Three Powers of the Soul".

The Book of Keys, "The Virtues of Gratitude and Magnanimity".

21: *The Book of Keys*, "Escaping from Contingency".

22: *The Book of Keys*, "What I Must Do".

The Book of Keys, "Presence and Remembrance".

23: *The Book of Keys*, "The Four Key-Notions".

Spiritual Perspectives and Human Facts, "The Spiritual Virtues".

Light on the Ancient Worlds, "Man in the Universe".

24: *The Book of Keys*, "When Is a Disposition of the Soul Holy?"

25: *The Book of Keys*, "Character Is a Part of Intelligence".

The Book of Keys, "Serenity and Certitude".

26: *Logic and Transcendence*, "Oriental Dialectic and Its Roots in Faith".

Understanding Islam (Bloomington, IN: World Wisdom, 2011), "Islam".

27: *Light on the Ancient Worlds*, "Fall and Forfeiture".

The Transcendent Unity of Religions, "To Be Man Is To Know".

Survey of Metaphysics and Esoterism, "Epistemological Premises".

28: *The Transcendent Unity of Religions,* "To Be Man Is To Know".

Sufism: Veil and Quintessence, "Preface".

Sufism: Veil and Quintessence, "Paradoxes of an Esoterism".

From the Divine to the Human, "Outline of a Spiritual Anthropology".

29: *The Eye of the Heart* (Bloomington, IN: World Wisdom, 1997), "Modes of Spiritual Realization".

30: *The Book of Keys,* "Description of the Fundamental Virtues".

Stations of Wisdom, "Complexity of the Concept of Charity".

The Book of Keys, "Profane Illusions".

Stations of Wisdom, "Complexity of the Concept of Charity".

31: *The Book of Keys,* "What We Are Responsible For".

The Book of Keys, "On the Divine Nature".

32: *The Book of Keys*, "Man Is Able To Know, To Will, To Love".

The Book of Keys, "There Is Only One Religion".

The Book of Keys, "The Alchemy of the Microcosm results from the Theme of Identity".

33: *Light on the Ancient Worlds*, "The Universality and Timeliness of Monasticism".

The Book of Keys, "Where thy treasure is, there will thy heart be also".

Survey of Metaphysics and Esoterism, "Enigma and Message of an Esoterism".

The Book of Keys, "The Way of Trust and Mercy".

34: *The Book of Keys*, "The Four Predispositions".

Logic and Transcendence, "The Argument Founded on Substance".

Castes and Races (Bedfont: Perennial Books, 1959), "The Meaning of Race".

Spiritual Perspectives and Human Facts, "Knowledge and Love".

Spiritual Perspectives and Human Facts, "Contours of the Spirit".

35: *The Book of Keys*, "To Love Light and Air".

The Book of Keys, "Recollectedness, Inwardness, Remembrance of God".

Survey of Metaphysics and Esoterism, "Synthesis and Conclusion".

From the Divine to the Human, "Outline of a Spiritual Anthropology".

36: *The Book of Keys*, "There Is Only One Religion".

The Transcendent Unity of Religions, "To Be Man Is To Know".

Esoterism as Principle and as Way, "Criteria of Worth".

The Book of Keys, "Perfection of Faith".

Esoterism as Principle and as Way, "Foundations of an Integral Aesthetics".

37: *Spiritual Perspectives and Human Facts*, "Aesthetics and Symbolism in Art and Nature".

Spiritual Perspectives and Human Facts, "Aesthetics and Symbolism in Art and Nature".

The Book of Keys, "The Four Predispositions".

The Book of Keys, "The Four Predispositions".

38: *The Book of Keys*, "*Istihdhār* and *Hudhūr*".

Understanding Islam, "The Koran and the *Sunnah*".

Logic and Transcendence, "The Argument Founded on Substance".

39: *From the Divine to the Human*, "Structure and Universality of the Conditions of Existence".

From the Divine to the Human, "To Refuse or To Accept Revelation".

Understanding Islam, "The Path".

Spiritual Perspectives and Human Facts, "Contours of the Spirit".

40: *The Book of Keys*, "The Way Is Based on What Is Certain and Necessary".

The Book of Keys, "Having the Right Intention".

41: *Logic and Transcendence*, "Man and Certainty".

The Book of Keys, "Being Happy".

42: *The Book of Keys*, "The Two Great Moments".

Logic and Transcendence, "Man and Certainty".

43: *Roots of the Human Condition*, "Cosmic Shadows and Serenity".

44: *Esoterism as Principle and as Way*, "Dimensions of the Human Vocation".

Esoterism as Principle and as Way, "Dimensions of the Human Vocation".

The Book of Keys, "To Invoke With What We Have and With What We Are".

Spiritual Perspectives and Human Facts, "Knowledge and Love".

45: *Sufism: Veil and Quintessence*, "Paradoxes of an Esoterism".

The Book of Keys, "Knowing, Willing, Loving God".

Survey of Metaphysics and Esoterism, "Epistemological Premises".

46: *Logic and Transcendence*, "The Problem of Qualifications".

Survey of Metaphysics and Esoterism, "Confessional Speculations: Intentions and Impasses".

The Book of Keys, "The Doctrine of the Thematic Unfolding".

From the Divine to the Human, "To Refuse or To Accept Revelation".

47: *The Book of Keys,* "Faith Is To Say 'Yes'".

The Book of Keys, "Faith Is To Say 'Yes'".

From the Divine to the Human, "The Interplay of the Hypostases".

The Eye of the Heart, "On Knowledge".

Spiritual Perspectives and Human Facts, "The Spiritual Virtues".

48: *Spiritual Perspectives and Human Facts,* "The Spiritual Virtues".

Christianity/Islam: Perspectives on Esoteric Ecumenism (Bloomington, IN: World Wisdom, 2008), "The Question of Protestantism".

From the Divine to the Human, "To Refuse or To Accept Revelation".

The Book of Keys, "The Way of Trust and Mercy".

49: *The Book of Keys*, "The Four Predispositions".

The Book of Keys, "The Four Predispositions".

The Book of Keys, "The Substance".

From the Divine to the Human, "To Refuse or To Accept Revelation".

50: *The Book of Keys*, "The Three Powers of the Soul".

The Book of Keys, "The Six Fundamental Givens".

Understanding Islam, "The Koran and the *Sunnah*".

51: *Esoterism as Principle and as Way*, "The Triple Nature of Man".

The Book of Keys, "Spiritual Sleep".

52: Letter of 15 September 1984.

Sufism: Veil and Quintessence, "Paradoxes of an Esoterism".

Personal notebook, 1953.

Stations of Wisdom, "Modes of Prayer".

--- ∴ ---

53: *To Have a Center*, "Fundamental Keys".

Survey of Metaphysics and Esoterism, "The Irrefutable Religion".

54: *The Book of Keys*, "The Epistle of the Choice and of the Triple Destiny".

Spiritual Perspectives and Human Facts, "The Spiritual Virtues".

Stations of Wisdom, "Modes of Prayer".

55: *Stations of Wisdom*, "Modes of Prayer".

In the Face of the Absolute, "Preface".

56: *The Book of Keys*, "The Only Question That Matters".

57: *The Book of Keys*, "The Way Is Simple".

58-59: *The Book of Keys*, "The Open Gate".

59: *The Book of Keys*, "The Open Gate".

60-61: *The Book of Keys*, "Objectivity: Intellective, Volitive, and Affective".

61: *Esoterism as Principle and as Way*, "The Triple Nature of Man".

———— ·:· ————

The Book of Keys, "Objectivity: Intellective, Volitive, and Affective".

62: *The Book of Keys,* "Gratitude and Generosity".

63: *The Book of Keys,* "Self-Knowledge and Generosity".

64: *The Book of Keys,* "Poverty".

65: *The Book of Keys,* "Combating the Faults of the Soul".

66: *The Book of Keys,* "Beyond Dissonances".

67: *The Book of Keys,* "Character Is a Part of Intelligence".

68: *The Book of Keys,* "Beauty's Requirement".

The Book of Keys, "Keeping a Balance".

69: *Roots of the Human Condition,* "Pillars of Wisdom".

Roots of the Human Condition, "Pillars of Wisdom".

Roots of the Human Condition, "Pillars of Wisdom".

70: *The Book of Keys,* "From the Form to the Essence".

71: *From the Divine to the Human,* "The Sense of the Sacred".

<hr />

The Book of Keys, "Keeping a Balance".

72: *The Book of Keys*, "Truth, Peace, Beauty".

73: *The Book of Keys*, "Moral Realism".

74: *The Book of Keys*, "Being Right Is Not Everything".

75: *Vincit omnia veritas* (Latin): "Truth conquers all".

The Book of Keys, "Maintaining Oneself in Peace".

76: *The Book of Keys*, "On Some Vices Found in Human Societies".

77: *The Book of Keys*, "Outwardness and Matter".

78: *The Book of Keys*, "Inwardness Equals Certitude and Peace".

79: *The Book of Keys*, "Being Alone With God".

80-81: *The Book of Keys*, "Against Subtle Worldliness".

82-83: *The Book of Keys*, "The Criteria of the Spiritual Man".

84: *The Book of Keys*, "No Worship without Respect".

85: *Logic and Transcendence*, "Man and Certainty".

—— ⫶ ——

86: *Religio perennis* (Latin): "perennial religion".

Light on the Ancient Worlds, "*Religio Perennis*".

Roots of the Human Condition, "*Mahāshakti*".

87: *The Book of Keys*, "Notion of the Absolute, Love of God".

Esoterism as Principle and as Way, "Understanding Esoterism".

88: *Stations of Wisdom*, "Modes of Prayer".

89: *Understanding Islam*, "Islam".

Spiritual Perspectives and Human Facts, "The Spiritual Virtues".

Selections from Letters and Other Previously Unpublished Writings

93: *Primordial Meditation: Contemplating the Real*, First Collection, *Sacred Web*, vol. 20, Winter 2007.

Primordial Meditation: Contemplating the Real, Third Collection.

94: *Primordial Meditation: Contemplating the Real*, Fourth Collection.

---------- ⋅⋅⋅ ----------

The Book of Keys, "God Is the Good".

95: Letter of 3 November 1950.

96: Letter of 13 January 1957.

Memories and Meditations, "Journey to America 1959". "Schuon kept notebooks during his life as an *aide mémoire* without any intention of having them published. However, in the early 1970s he collected and edited his notebooks and travel journals in response to repeated requests from his friends. . . . The resultant work, entitled *Erinnerungen und Betrachtungen* ("Memories and Meditations"), was privately circulated in 1974. . . . By his own wishes they remain unpublished to this day" (Michael Fitzgerald, *Frithjof Schuon: Messenger of the Perennial Philosophy* [Bloomington, IN: World Wisdom, 2010], pp. 173-174).

97: Letter of 23 April 1962.

98: *Memories and Meditations*, "Journey to America 1963".

99: Letter of 19 December 1963.

100: Letter of 3 April 1969.

101: Letter of 9 September 1969.

From an undated letter.

—— ·:· ——

102: "Message to the Colloquium", in *Traditional Modes of Contemplation and Action: A Colloquium held at Rothko Chapel, Houston Texas*, ed. Yusuf Ibish & Peter Lamborn Wilson (Tehran: Imperial Iranian Academy of Philosophy, 1977). A version of this message was later revised and included in *The Play of Masks* (Bloomington, IN: World Wisdom, 1992) as the chapter "No Initiative without Truth".

103: *Vincit omnia Veritas* (Latin): "Truth conquers all".

Letter of 24 December 1980.

104-5: From a letter, circa 1982.

105: *The Transfiguration of Man*, "Dimensions of Prayer".

Private paper, "Conditions of Certitude", circa 1986.

106: "Envoy of God" is one of the titles of the Prophet Muhammad, although Schuon's comments could also be applied to the Christ, Moses, or any of the founders of the great religions.

106-7: Letter of 28 March 1985.

108: Response to a question, circa 1985.

Letter of 21 January 1986.

---- ⁙ ----

109: From a note, circa 1990.

110: *The Transfiguration of Man,* "Axioms of the *Sophia Perennis*".

111: *The Book of Keys,* "Hope and Faith".

BIOGRAPHICAL NOTES

Frithjof Schuon

Born in Basle, Switzerland in 1907, Frithjof Schuon was the twentieth century's pre-eminent spokesman for the perennialist school of comparative religious thought.

The leitmotif of Schuon's work was foreshadowed in an encounter during his youth with a marabout who had accompanied some members of his Senegalese village to Basle for the purpose of demonstrating their African culture. When Schuon talked with him, the venerable old man drew a circle with radii on the ground and explained: "God is the center; all paths lead to Him." Until his later years Schuon traveled widely, from India and the Middle East to America, experiencing traditional cultures and establishing lifelong friendships with Hindu, Buddhist, Christian, Muslim, and American Indian spiritual leaders.

A philosopher in the tradition of Plato, Shankara, and Eckhart, Schuon was a gifted artist and poet as well as the author of over twenty books on religion, metaphysics, sacred art, and the spiritual path. Describing his first book, *The Transcendent Unity of Religions*, T. S. Eliot wrote, "I have met with no more impressive work in the comparative study of Oriental and Occidental religion", and world-renowned religion scholar Huston Smith said of Schuon, "The man is a living wonder; intellectually apropos religion, equally in depth and breadth, the paragon

—— ·ː· ——

of our time". Schuon's books have been translated into over a dozen languages and are respected by academic and religious authorities alike.

More than a scholar and writer, Schuon was a spiritual guide for seekers from a wide variety of religions and backgrounds throughout the world. He died in the United States in 1998.

Patrick Casey served as an aide and secretary to Frithjof Schuon for over 20 years. After earning a degree in Religious Studies from Indiana University in 1975, Casey traveled to Switzerland to meet Schuon for the first time. In the early 1980s, after Schuon had moved to America, Casey approached him with the idea of collecting the letters he had sent over the years to correspondents in America, England, Germany, Switzerland, and elsewhere. With Schuon's approval, Casey began a process that resulted in the collection of more than 1,500 letters; many of these have since been published in various works, while some appear for the first time in the Appendix to the present book. Today, Casey lives near Schuon's former home in Bloomington, Indiana, and is married to Jennifer Casey, the director of two film documentaries: *Native Spirit & The Sun Dance Way* (2007) and *Frithjof Schuon: Messenger of the Perennial Philosophy* (2012). They have two adult children.

Adastra & Stella Maris:
Poems by Frithjof Schuon (bilingual edition)
Autumn Leaves & The Ring:
Poems by Frithjof Schuon (bilingual edition)
Songs without Names, Volumes I-VI: Poems by Frithjof Schuon
Songs without Names, Volumes VII-XII: Poems by Frithjof Schuon
World Wheel, Volumes I-III: Poems by Frithjof Schuon
World Wheel, Volumes IV-VII: Poems by Frithjof Schuon
Primordial Meditation: Contemplating the Real

Edited Writings

The Essential Frithjof Schuon, ed. Seyyed Hossein Nasr
Songs for a Spiritual Traveler: Selected Poems (bilingual edition)
René Guénon: Some Observations, ed. William Stoddart
The Fullness of God: Frithjof Schuon on Christianity,
ed. James S. Cutsinger
Prayer Fashions Man: Frithjof Schuon on the Spiritual Life,
ed. James S. Cutsinger
Art from the Sacred to the Profane: East and West,
ed. Catherine Schuon
Splendor of the True: A Frithjof Schuon Reader,
ed. James S. Cutsinger (forthcoming)